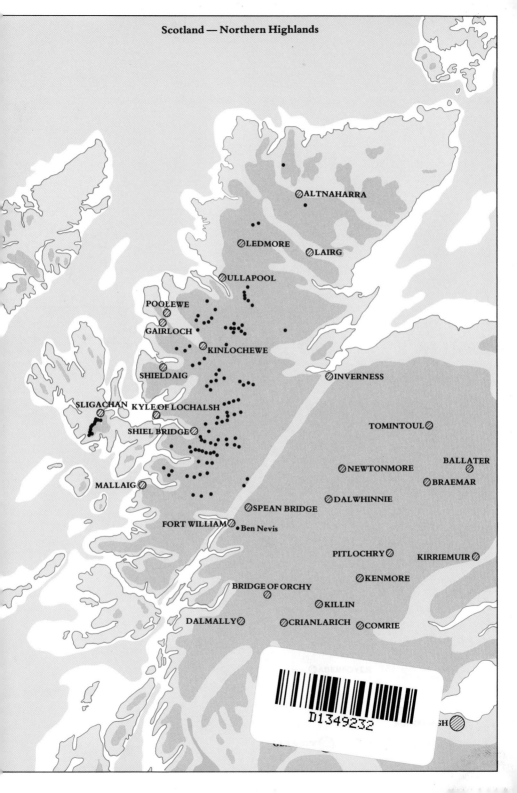

# Scotland — Northern Highlands

# A MUNROIST'S LOG

Published by the Ernest Press 1992
© Copyright Irvine Butterfield/Jack Baines

Reprinted 2003 with amendment

British Library Cataloguing-in-Publication Data
  Butterfield Irvine, 1936-
  Munroist's Log.
  I. Title
  796.522

ISBN 0 948153 14 8

*Line drawings, Euan McArthur*

Typeset by EMS Phototypesetting, Berwick on Tweed, in 10pt Plantin
Printed by Kyodo Ptg. Co.

# *A MUNROIST'S LOG*

*Being a log in which to record ascents
of those mountains in an extended list
of 3000 ft summits in the British Isles.*

**Researched by Irvine Butterfield
from an idea by Jack Baines**

# CONTENTS

What is a Munro............................................................... 6

Sir Hugh T. Munro............................................................ 6

Odd facts about Munros and the 3000ft peaks ................................ 7

The first among Munroists ..................................................... 8

The 3000ft mountains with 250ft of ascent on all sides ...................... 9

## LOG SHEETS

| | | |
|---|---|---|
| Section 1 | Lomond, Arrochar, Crianlarich and Tyndrum Hills .... | 11 |
| Section 2 | Loch Earn and Crieff ......................................... | 21 |
| Section 3 | Rannoch, Lyon, Lochay and Bridge of Orchy Hills...... | 24 |
| Section 4 | Cruachan, Etive, Black Mount, South Glencoe and Appin ...................................................... | 39 |
| Section 5 | North Glencoe, Nether Lochaber, Alder and West Drumochter........................................ | 51 |
| Section 6 | Loch Laggan and the Monadh Liath....................... | 73 |
| Section 7 | Lochy, Arkaig, Knoydart, Quoich and South Glen Shiel.............................................. | 80 |
| Section 8 | Kintail, Ceannacroc and Affric ............................ | 94 |
| Section 9 | Cannich, Strathfarrar, Monar and Glen Carron........... | 106 |
| Section 10 | The Torridons ................................................ | 115 |
| Section 11 | Slioch, Fisherfield, Dundonell and the Fannaichs ....... | 120 |
| Section 12 | Wyvis, Strathvaick, Inverlael ............................. | 131 |
| Section 13 | Assynt and the far north..................................... | 136 |
| Section 14 | The Cairngorms ............................................. | 139 |
| Section 15 | Gaick, Atholl, Glen Ey and the Cairnwell ................. | 152 |
| Section 16 | Lochnagar and east of the Devil's Elbow.................. | 162 |
| Section 17 | Skye and Mull............................................... | 170 |

# RESEARCH AND DATA

Appendix A    Tables of 3000ft mountains with 250ft of ascent
on all sides ...................................................... 178

Appendix B    Log sheets for those peaks in Appendix A marked
with an asterix..................................................... 189

Appendix C    3000ft peaks with 250ft of reascent on all sides not
listed in Munro's Tables 1980-1990 ........................ 208

Tops promoted in 1980 revision of Munro's
Tables (Brown/Donaldson) ................................ 216

Mountains demoted to tops in Munro's
Tables 1980 (Brown/Donaldson revision) ................. 217

Heights classed as mountains in Munro's original
list not elsewhere recorded.................................. 219

Mountains listed in Munro's Tables 1980-1990
which fail to qualify under 250ft rule....................... 220

Furth of Scotland ............................................................ 223

Log sheets:    England ..................................................... 225

Wales ........................................................ 228

Ireland ....................................................... 233

Summary of mountains with 250ft of ascent on all sides...................... 238

Notes.................................................................... 239/40

# What is a Munro

The term Munro is applied to mountains in Scotland over 3000ft of which there are 277. The name is an eponymous one taken from the original compiler of the list of 3000ft peaks in Scotland, Sir Hugh Thomas Munro Bart., of Lindertis.

# Sir Hugh T. Munro

Sir Hugh Munro was the eldest of nine children and as such inherited his father's estate at Lindertis near Kirriemuir in Scotland. He was much travelled and, having first climbed mountains in Germany, was naturally attracted to his native hills. His enthusiasm led him to catalogue the 3000ft peaks, which up to that time were thought to number only some 30. It was Joseph Gibson Stott, first editor of the Scottish Mountaineering Club Journal, who claimed in the first publication of 1890 that there were more than 300 mountains in Scotland over 3000ft – no one at that time had fully explored the country the better to document them. Munro's list duly appeared in the 1891 edition of that same Journal, and from that time the term "Munro" gradually crept into the mountaineering vocabulary. This is somewhat ironic for Munro himself disliked eponymous names.

He was a founder member of the S.M.C. and was their third President. By a sad stroke of misfortune he was unable to arrange a suitable time when companions and weather came harmoniously together to allow ascent of the Inaccessible Pinnacle of Sgurr Dearg in Skye. He had also allowed Carn Cloich-mhuilinn to remain unclimbed as it was his intention to leave this mountain until last so that a leisurely ascent in the company of his friends could be made. The ease of ascent would also allow a pony to carry a hamper to the summit to mark the occasion with suitable celebration. Unfortunately he contracted a severe bout of pneumonia from which he never recovered and passed away at the age of 63, his one great ambition unfulfilled.

# Odd facts about Munros and the 3000ft peaks

Most northerly Munro, and 3000ft peak in the British Isles, is Ben Hope (3042ft/927m).

The most easterly Munro, and 3000ft peak in the British Isles, is Mount Keen (3077ft/939m).

The most southerly Munro is Ben Lomond (3192ft/974m).

The most westerly Munro is Sgurr na Banachdich (3167ft/965m) of the Cuillin in Skye.

The most westerly Munro on the Scottish mainland is Ladhar Bheinn (3343ft/1020m) in Knoydart.

The most southerly 3000ft peak in the British Isles is Cnoc an Chuilinn (3141ft/957m) of Macgillycuddy's Reeks in County Kerry, Ireland.

The most westerly 3000ft peak in the British Isles is Brandon Mountain (3127ft/953m) in County Kerry, Ireland.

The highest mountain in Munro's list, Ben Nevis (4406ft/1344m), is also the highest mountain in Britain and Ireland.

The highest mountain in England is Scafell Pike (3162ft/977m).

The highest mountain in Wales is Snowdon (3560ft/1085m).

The highest mountain in Ireland is Carrauntoohil (3414ft/1040m) of Macgillycuddy's Reeks, in County Kerry.

# The first among Munroists

The very first to ascend all the Munros was the Reverend Archibald Eneas Robertson, minister of the parish of Rannoch in Perthshire, who completed the round in 1901.

The Reverend A.R.G. Burn, the second person to complete the round in 1923, also claimed a first ascent of all the "tops".

The first to complete the Munros and the 3000ft peaks in England, Wales, and Ireland was J.A. Parker in 1929. He completed the Munros in 1927, being the third so to do.

The first Englishman to complete the round, John Rooke Corbett, also emulated the feat of the Reverend A.R.G. Burn by simultaneously completing the "tops" in 1930 to become the fourth Munroist. Corbett was a member of the Rucksack Club, and is credited with drawing up the list of the English and Welsh "25s", which appeared in the pages of their Journal. He also drew up a list of the Scottish 2500ft peaks and made ascents of them all.

The first to complete the grand slam of all the Munro "tops" and the English, Welsh and Irish 3000ft peaks was W.M. Docharty in 1949. He entered the Munros list as the thirteenth to complete.

The first lady to complete was Mrs Hirst in 1947. By so doing she also became, with her spouse, the first husband and wife team to complete the round, including the tops.

The first father and son to complete the round were J.Y. and C.G. MacDonald in 1958.

The first to complete a second round was Philip N.L. Tranter in 1964, having first completed in 1961.

The first to do the Munros in a single round was Hamish M. Brown in 1974, covering an estimated 1639 miles and climbing some 449,000 feet on an ascent of 289 peaks in 112 days. He also holds the record for the highest number of Munro rounds.

The first lady to complete in a single round was Kathy Murgatroyd in 1982.

The first to complete in a single round in winter was Martin Moran in 1985, taking 83 days.

# The 3000ft mountains
## (With 250ft of ascent on all sides)

The revision of "Munro's Tables" in 1980 saw the deletion of 7 mountains – Carn Ballach (3020ft/920m), Carn Ban (3087ft/942m), Carn Ban Mor (3443ft/1052m), Geal-Charn (3019ft/920m), Meall Dubhag (3268ft/998m), Carn Cloich-mhuilinn (3087ft/942m), and A'Choinneach (3345ft/1017m).

None save A'Choinneach have 250ft of ascent on all sides, A'Choinneach achieving this by the merest margin of 2ft at the col separating it from Bynack More.

The 4 tops (Sgor an Iubhair (3284ft/1001m), Garbh Chioch Mhor (3365ft/1013m), Mullach an Rathain (3358ft/1023m), and Sgurr Fiona (3474ft/1059m) revised to mountain status all had 250ft of ascent on all sides: the latter two adding to the overall stature of their respective mountains, Liathach and An Teallach. The further addition of Sgurr nan Ceannaichean (2896ft/915m), and the later addition of Beinn Teallach (2994ft/915) in 1990, were justified on similar grounds: their summit heights having finally been confirmed as exceeding 3000ft.

The deletions, it could be argued, were in the spirit of Munro's observation that "In the Eastern Grampians it is specially difficult to decide what are separate mountains". Those tops revised to mountain status were less easy to explain when set against a firm criteria, which many felt would better merit so complete a revision of Munro's Tables.

When Corbett published his list of 2500ft mountains at a later date, he adopted a criteria of 500ft of ascent on all sides. From an analysis of Munro's original amendments, there is a hint that a similar judgement was possibly in the mind of Munro, with 250ft of re-ascent on all sides the most probable factor considered. Bearing in mind that the maps used by Munro were some of the earliest 1″ and 6″ maps of the Ordnance Survey, published in the late nineteenth century, it is not surprising that some of the definitions of an indistinctly, or inaccurately, recorded topography gave him pause for thought; and the status of peaks was reconsidered.

Given the advances in surveying technique, it is not unusual to find that the more clearly defined contours of the current 1:50 000 and 1:25 000 maps of the present day confirm Munro's original assessments. When the 250ft of ascent on all sides criteria is adopted, some interesting facts now emerge. Of the tops which would then fall to be classified as mountains, it is seen that several of Munro's original mountains, revised to tops in 1921 editions of the Tables, would revert to mountain status. These are Beinn Iutharn Bheag (3121ft/953m), Bidean an Eoin Deirg (3430ft/1046m), Creag Dubh (3102ft/946m), Sgor Choinnich (3040ft/ 929m), Sgor an Lochain Uaine (Angel's Peak) (4150ft/1258m), and Sgurr na Lapaich (Mam Sodhail) (3401ft/1036m).

The Tables of mountains with 250ft of ascent on all sides would show that, were such a definition to be adopted, there would be 304 such mountains in Scotland. These Tables are given in Appendix A.

An asterisk is used to denote those peaks which are not classified as mountains in the revised Munro's lists of 1980-1990, but would qualify to be listed as mountains fulfilling the criteria of having 250ft of ascent on all sides. Those wishing to pursue the additional goal inferred by these Tables, will find the log sheets for these mountains in Appendix B: those with an enquiring, or sceptical mind, can examine parts of the author's research data in Appendix C.

N.B. – The imperial heights used throughout are those from the last editions of the O.S. one inch to one mile maps. In many cases there is not an exact relationship between the old imperial and current metric heights.

## Note for the 2003 edition

An asterisk is used to denote those peaks which are not classified as mountain in *Munro's Tables* of 1980-1990, but would qualify to be listed as mountains fulfilling the criteria of having 250 ft of ascent on all sides. See log sheets for these mountains in Appendix B and examine research data in Appendix C.

A plus sign is used to denote those peaks which were reclassified as mountains in *Munro's Tables* of 1997. A dagger sign is used to denote the peak which was demoted to a Top in *Munro's Tables* of 1997.

# 1 Lomond, Arrochar, Crianlarich and Tyndrum Hills

*Beinn Laoigh*

## Ben Lomond                                              3192ft/974m

Beacon Mountain

Distance_____ Miles/Km  Height_____ ft/m  Date___/___/___

Weather _____

Companions _____

Route _____

and Notes _____

_____

_____

_____

_____

_____

_____

_____


## Beinn Narnain                                           3036ft/926m

Origin unknown

Distance_____ Miles/Km  Height_____ ft/m  Date___/___/___

Weather _____

Companions _____

Route _____

and Notes _____

_____

_____

_____

_____

_____

_____

_____

| **Beinn Ime** | **3318ft/1011m** |

The butter mountain

Distance_____ Miles/Km    Height_____ ft/m    Date_____/_____/_____

Weather    _____

Companions    _____

Route    _____

and Notes    _____

_____

_____

_____

_____

_____

_____

_____

_____


| **Ben Vane** | **3004ft/916m** |

The white, or middle mountain

Distance_____ Miles/Km    Height_____ ft/m    Date_____/_____/_____

Weather    _____

Companions    _____

Route    _____

and Notes    _____

_____

_____

_____

_____

_____

_____

_____

| **Beinn an Lochain** | **3021ft/901m** |
|---|---|

The mountain of the little loch

Distance_____ Miles/Km   Height_____ ft/m   Date____/____/____

Weather _____

Companions _____

Route _____

and Notes _____

_____

_____

_____

_____

_____

The highest point recorded on the 1″ maps of the Ordnance Survey was 2995ft, later reduced to 2992ft. The summit was said to be 150 yards N.E. of this spot height. The revision of the Ordnance Survey maps led to the deletion of this mountain from the 1980 issue of Munro's Tables.

| **Ben Vorlich** | **3092ft/943m** |
|---|---|

Height of the sea-bag

Distance_____ Miles/Km   Height_____ ft/m   Date____/____/____

Weather _____

Companions _____

Route _____

and Notes _____

_____

_____

_____

_____

_____

_____

_____

| **Beinn Bhuidhe** | **3106ft/948m** |
|---|---|

The yellow mountain

Distance_____ Miles/Km  Height_____ ft/m  Date____/____/____

Weather _____

Companions _____

Route _____

and Notes _____

_____

_____

_____

_____

_____

_____

_____

_____

| **Beinn a'Chleibh** | **3008ft/917m** |
|---|---|

Hill of the chest

Distance_____ Miles/Km  Height_____ ft/m  Date____/____/____

Weather _____

Companions _____

Route _____

and Notes _____

_____

_____

_____

_____

_____

_____

_____

| **Beinn Laoigh (Ben Lui)** | **3708ft/1130m** |

Mountain of the calf

Distance_____ Miles/Km   Height_____ ft/m   Date____/____/____

Weather      _____

Companions   _____

Route        _____

and Notes    _____

_____

_____

_____

_____

_____

_____

_____

_____

| **Ben Oss** | **3374ft/1028m** |

Mountain of the elk, or stag

Distance_____ Miles/Km   Height_____ ft/m   Date____/____/____

Weather      _____

Companions   _____

Route        _____

and Notes    _____

_____

_____

_____

_____

_____

_____

_____

_____

_____

## Beinn Dubhchraig                                      3204ft/977m
Mountain of the black rock

Distance_____ Miles/Km  Height_____ ft/m  Date____/____/____

Weather      _____

Companions   _____

Route        _____

and Notes    _____

_____

_____

_____

_____

_____

_____

_____

## Beinn Chabhair                                       3053ft/931m
The mountain of the antler, or hawk

Distance_____ Miles/Km  Height_____ ft/m  Date____/____/____

Weather      _____

Companions   _____

Route        _____

and Notes    _____

_____

_____

_____

_____

_____

_____

_____

17

## An Caisteal                                                3265ft/995m
The castle

Distance_____ Miles/Km   Height_____ ft/m   Date____/____/____
Weather         _____
Companions      _____
Route           _____
and Notes       _____

_____
_____
_____
_____
_____
_____
_____
_____

## Beinn a'Chroin                                             3104ft/940m
Mountain of harm, or danger

Distance_____ Miles/Km   Height_____ ft/m   Date____/____/____
Weather         _____
Companions      _____
Route           _____
and Notes       _____

_____
_____
_____
_____
_____
_____
_____
_____

18

## Beinn Tulaichean                                                    3099ft/945m
*The knolly mountain*

Distance＿＿＿＿＿ Miles/Km   Height＿＿＿＿＿ ft/m   Date＿＿/＿＿/＿＿

Weather     ＿＿＿＿＿＿＿＿＿＿＿＿＿＿＿＿＿＿＿＿＿＿＿＿＿＿＿＿＿

Companions  ＿＿＿＿＿＿＿＿＿＿＿＿＿＿＿＿＿＿＿＿＿＿＿＿＿＿＿＿＿

Route       ＿＿＿＿＿＿＿＿＿＿＿＿＿＿＿＿＿＿＿＿＿＿＿＿＿＿＿＿＿

and Notes   ＿＿＿＿＿＿＿＿＿＿＿＿＿＿＿＿＿＿＿＿＿＿＿＿＿＿＿＿＿

＿＿＿＿＿＿＿＿＿＿＿＿＿＿＿＿＿＿＿＿＿＿＿＿＿＿＿＿＿＿＿＿＿＿＿＿＿

＿＿＿＿＿＿＿＿＿＿＿＿＿＿＿＿＿＿＿＿＿＿＿＿＿＿＿＿＿＿＿＿＿＿＿＿＿

＿＿＿＿＿＿＿＿＿＿＿＿＿＿＿＿＿＿＿＿＿＿＿＿＿＿＿＿＿＿＿＿＿＿＿＿＿

＿＿＿＿＿＿＿＿＿＿＿＿＿＿＿＿＿＿＿＿＿＿＿＿＿＿＿＿＿＿＿＿＿＿＿＿＿

＿＿＿＿＿＿＿＿＿＿＿＿＿＿＿＿＿＿＿＿＿＿＿＿＿＿＿＿＿＿＿＿＿＿＿＿＿

＿＿＿＿＿＿＿＿＿＿＿＿＿＿＿＿＿＿＿＿＿＿＿＿＿＿＿＿＿＿＿＿＿＿＿＿＿

＿＿＿＿＿＿＿＿＿＿＿＿＿＿＿＿＿＿＿＿＿＿＿＿＿＿＿＿＿＿＿＿＿＿＿＿＿

## Cruach Ardrain                                                    3248ft/1045m
*The high heap or mountain*

Distance＿＿＿＿＿ Miles/Km   Height＿＿＿＿＿ ft/m   Date＿＿/＿＿/＿＿

Weather     ＿＿＿＿＿＿＿＿＿＿＿＿＿＿＿＿＿＿＿＿＿＿＿＿＿＿＿＿＿

Companions  ＿＿＿＿＿＿＿＿＿＿＿＿＿＿＿＿＿＿＿＿＿＿＿＿＿＿＿＿＿

Route       ＿＿＿＿＿＿＿＿＿＿＿＿＿＿＿＿＿＿＿＿＿＿＿＿＿＿＿＿＿

and Notes   ＿＿＿＿＿＿＿＿＿＿＿＿＿＿＿＿＿＿＿＿＿＿＿＿＿＿＿＿＿

＿＿＿＿＿＿＿＿＿＿＿＿＿＿＿＿＿＿＿＿＿＿＿＿＿＿＿＿＿＿＿＿＿＿＿＿＿

＿＿＿＿＿＿＿＿＿＿＿＿＿＿＿＿＿＿＿＿＿＿＿＿＿＿＿＿＿＿＿＿＿＿＿＿＿

＿＿＿＿＿＿＿＿＿＿＿＿＿＿＿＿＿＿＿＿＿＿＿＿＿＿＿＿＿＿＿＿＿＿＿＿＿

＿＿＿＿＿＿＿＿＿＿＿＿＿＿＿＿＿＿＿＿＿＿＿＿＿＿＿＿＿＿＿＿＿＿＿＿＿

＿＿＿＿＿＿＿＿＿＿＿＿＿＿＿＿＿＿＿＿＿＿＿＿＿＿＿＿＿＿＿＿＿＿＿＿＿

＿＿＿＿＿＿＿＿＿＿＿＿＿＿＿＿＿＿＿＿＿＿＿＿＿＿＿＿＿＿＿＿＿＿＿＿＿

＿＿＿＿＿＿＿＿＿＿＿＿＿＿＿＿＿＿＿＿＿＿＿＿＿＿＿＿＿＿＿＿＿＿＿＿＿

| **Ben More** | | | **3843ft/1174m** |
| --- | --- | --- | --- |

Big mountain

Distance_____ Miles/Km   Height_____ ft/m   Date\_\_\_/\_\_\_/\_\_\_

Weather  _____

Companions  _____

Route  _____

and Notes  _____

| **Stob Binnein (Stobinian)** | | | **3821ft/1165m** |
| --- | --- | --- | --- |

The pinnacle, or anvil peak

Distance_____ Miles/Km   Height_____ ft/m   Date\_\_\_/\_\_\_/\_\_\_

Weather  _____

Companions  _____

Route  _____

and Notes  _____

# 2   Loch Earn and Crieff

Ben Vorlich

## Ben Vorlich 3231ft/985m

Height of the sea-bag

Distance_____ Miles/Km    Height_____ ft/m    Date____/____/____

Weather         _____

Companions      _____

Route           _____

and Notes       _____

_____

_____

_____

_____

_____

_____

_____

_____


## Stuc a'Chroin 3189ft/972m

Peak of harm, or danger

Distance_____ Miles/Km    Height_____ ft/m    Date____/____/____

Weather         _____

Companions      _____

Route           _____

and Notes       _____

_____

_____

_____

_____

_____

_____

_____

22

## Ben Chonzie                                          3048ft/931m

The mountain of weeping

Distance_____ Miles/Km   Height_____ ft/m   Date____/____/____

Weather      _____

Companions   _____

Route        _____

and Notes    _____

_____

_____

_____

_____

_____

_____

_____

_____

_____

# 3 Rannoch, Lyon, Lochay and Bridge of Orchy hills

*Meall Buidhe and Beinn Achaladair*

| **Schiehallion** | **3547ft/1083m** |

The fairies' hill, or the fairy hill of the Caledonians

Distance_____ Miles/Km  Height_____ ft/m  Date____/____/____

Weather      _____

Companions   _____

Route        _____

and Notes    _____

_____

_____

_____

_____

_____

_____

_____

The glen behind Schiehallion is regarded by some as the heart of Scotland. Those patriots wishing to express a love of country often used the toast "Here's to the back o' Schiehallion".

Carn Mairg above Glen Lyon takes its name from a time when the plague swept up Glen Lyon. There is a tradition that of the village of Fortingall, the only survivors were an old woman and a white horse. The many who died are said to be buried under a cairn seen in the field in front of the thatched houses in the village, and this too is known as Carn na Marbh, the cairn of the dead.

Fortingall village is the reputed birthplace of Pontius Pilate and in the churchyard there is an old yew tree thought to be over three thousand years old.

## Carn Mairg                                        3419ft/1042m

Hill of sorrow, or the dead

Distance_____ Miles/Km   Height_____ ft/m   Date___/___/___

Weather        _____

Companions     _____

Route          _____

and Notes      _____

_____

_____

_____

_____

_____

_____

_____

_____


## Creag Mhor                                        3200ft/981m

Big crag

Distance_____ Miles/Km   Height_____ ft/m   Date___/___/___

Weather        _____

Companions     _____

Route          _____

and Notes      _____

_____

_____

_____

_____

_____

_____

_____

_____

## Carn Gorm                                            3370ft/1029m

Blue mountain

Distance_____ Miles/Km   Height_____ ft/m   Date____/____/____

Weather      _____

Companions   _____

Route        _____

and Notes    _____

_____

_____

_____

_____

_____

_____

_____

_____


## Meall Garbh                                          3200ft/963m

The rough, round hill

Distance_____ Miles/Km   Height_____ ft/m   Date____/____/____

Weather      _____

Companions   _____

Route        _____

and Notes    _____

_____

_____

_____

_____

_____

_____

_____

_____

27

## Ben Lawers                   3984ft/1214m

Loud, or hoof, or claw mountain

Distance_____ Miles/Km   Height_____ ft/m   Date\_\_\_/\_\_\_/\_\_\_

Weather _____

Companions _____

Route _____

and Notes _____

## Beinn Ghlas                   3657ft/1103m

The grey, or green mountain

Distance_____ Miles/Km   Height_____ ft/m   Date\_\_\_/\_\_\_/\_\_\_

Weather _____

Companions _____

Route _____

and Notes _____

## Meall Greigh                                     3280ft/1001m
The round hill of the cheek

Distance_____ Miles/Km  Height_____ ft/m  Date___/___/___

Weather    _____

Companions _____

Route      _____

and Notes  _____

_____

_____

_____

_____

_____

_____

_____

_____


## Meall Garbh                                      3661ft/1118m
The rough, round hill

Distance_____ Miles/Km  Height_____ ft/m  Date___/___/___

Weather    _____

Companions _____

Route      _____

and Notes  _____

_____

_____

_____

_____

_____

_____

_____

_____

## Meall Corranaich | 3530ft/1069m

The round hill of the corrie of bracken

Distance_____ Miles/Km   Height_____ ft/m   Date____/____/____

Weather _____

Companions _____

Route _____

and Notes _____

_____

_____

_____

_____

_____

_____

_____

_____


## Meall a'Choire Leith | 3033ft/926m

The round hill of the grey corrie

Distance_____ Miles/Km   Height_____ ft/m   Date____/____/____

Weather _____

Companions _____

Route _____

and Notes _____

_____

_____

_____

_____

_____

_____

_____

| **Meall nan Tarmachan** | **3421ft/1043m** |

The round hill of the ptarmigan

Distance_____ Miles/Km   Height_____ ft/m   Date\_\_\_/\_\_\_/\_\_\_

Weather _____

Companions _____

Route _____

and Notes _____

_____

_____

_____

_____

_____

_____

| **Meall Ghaordaidh** | **3410ft/1039m** |

Hill of the shoulder, arm, or hand

Distance_____ Miles/Km   Height_____ ft/m   Date\_\_\_/\_\_\_/\_\_\_

Weather _____

Companions _____

Route _____

and Notes _____

_____

_____

_____

_____

_____

_____

## Stuchd an Lochain                                    3144ft/960m

The peak of the little loch

Distance_____ Miles/Km   Height_____ ft/m   Date____/____/____

Weather       _____

Companions    _____

Route         _____

and Notes     _____

_____

_____

_____

_____

_____

_____

_____

_____


## Meall Buidhe                                          3054ft/931m

The rounded, yellow hill

Distance_____ Miles/Km   Height_____ ft/m   Date____/____/____

Weather       _____

Companions    _____

Route         _____

and Notes     _____

_____

_____

_____

_____

_____

_____

_____

_____

## Beinn Heasgarnich                                      3530ft/1076m
### The sheltering mountain

Distance_____ Miles/Km    Height_____ ft/m    Date____/____/____

Weather      _____

Companions   _____

Route        _____

and Notes    _____

_____

_____

_____

_____

_____

_____

_____

_____

_____


## Creag Mhor                                            3387ft/1032m
### The big crag

Distance_____ Miles/Km    Height_____ ft/m    Date____/____/____

Weather      _____

Companions   _____

Route        _____

and Notes    _____

_____

_____

_____

_____

_____

_____

_____

_____

## Ben Challum                                          3354ft/1022m
### Malcolm's mountain

Distance_____ Miles/Km   Height_____ ft/m   Date____/____/____

Weather        _____

Companions  _____

Route           _____

and Notes    _____

_____

_____

_____

_____

_____

_____

_____

_____


## Meall Glas                                           3139ft/957m
### The rounded grey hill

Distance_____ Miles/Km   Height_____ ft/m   Date____/____/____

Weather        _____

Companions  _____

Route           _____

and Notes    _____

_____

_____

_____

_____

_____

_____

_____

## Sgiath Chuil 3016ft/919m
The back wing

Distance_____ Miles/Km  Height_____ ft/m  Date____/____/____

Weather         _____

Companions      _____

Route           _____

and Notes       _____

_____

_____

_____

_____

_____

_____

_____

_____


## Beinn Dorain 3524ft/1074m
The mountain of the otter

Distance_____ Miles/Km  Height_____ ft/m  Date____/____/____

Weather         _____

Companions      _____

Route           _____

and Notes       _____

_____

_____

_____

_____

_____

_____

_____

## Beinn an Dothaidh                                    3289ft/1002m

The mountain of scorching

Distance_____ Miles/Km   Height_____ ft/m   Date____/____/____

Weather        _____

Companions    _____

Route          _____

and Notes      _____

_____

_____

_____

_____

_____

_____

_____


## Beinn Achaladair                                    3404ft/1038m

The mountain of the soaking field

Distance_____ Miles/Km   Height_____ ft/m   Date____/____/____

Weather        _____

Companions    _____

Route          _____

and Notes      _____

_____

_____

_____

_____

_____

_____

_____

## Beinn a'Chreachain          3540ft/1081m

The mountain of the plunderers (cattle lifters)

Distance_____ Miles/Km  Height_____ ft/m  Date\_\_\_/\_\_\_/\_\_\_

Weather      _____

Companions   _____

Route        _____

and Notes     _____

Beinn a'Chreachain takes its name from the reiving bands of Lochaber and Glen Coe who used the pass of the Lairig Mheuran when returning from Glen Lyon with their booty. In 1749 the military commander of a post at Tummel Bridge reported that watch was kept for thieves at the head of Glen Lyon, "a very remarkable pass to and from the Isle of Skye". The military station at the head of Loch Rannoch mentions the practice of "drovers returning from Crieff Fair stealing cattle from the Low Country, which they were accustomed to drive to the Highlands by the head of Loch Tay and Lion, and by the important pass at Carn half-way between this and Augh-Chalada, a large village near Dillebegg".

Beinn Mhanach takes its name from the monks who once resided at a small monastery at the mountain's foot between the head of Loch Lyon and Auch Gleann. This lay on a route often taken by the Glen Lyon MacGregors on their way to their clan burial ground at Glenorchy church.

| **Beinn Mhanach** | **3125ft/953m** |

The monk's mountain

Distance_____ Miles/Km   Height_____ ft/m   Date____/____/____

Weather   _____

Companions   _____

Route   _____

and Notes   _____

_____

_____

_____

_____

_____

_____

_____

_____

_____

# 4 Cruachan, Etive, Black Mount, South Glencoe and Appin

*Drochaid Ghlas, Ben Cruachan and Stob Dearg*

## Ben Cruachan                    3695ft/1126m

Mountain of peaks

Distance_____ Miles/Km   Height_____ ft/m   Date___/___/___

Weather _____

Companions _____

Route _____

and Notes _____

_____

_____

_____

_____

_____

_____

_____

_____

## Stob Diamh                    3272ft/997m

Peak of the stags

Distance_____ Miles/Km   Height_____ ft/m   Date___/___/___

Weather _____

Companions _____

Route _____

and Notes _____

_____

_____

_____

_____

_____

_____

_____

_____

## Beinn a'Chochuill | 3215ft/980m
Mountain of the hood

Distance_____ Miles/Km  Height_____ ft/m  Date____/____/____

Weather _____

Companions _____

Route _____

and Notes _____

_____

_____

_____

_____

_____

_____

_____

_____


## Beinn Eunaich | 3242ft/988m
Fowling mountain

Distance_____ Miles/Km  Height_____ ft/m  Date____/____/____

Weather _____

Companions _____

Route _____

and Notes _____

_____

_____

_____

_____

_____

_____

_____

_____

## Ben Starav                                           3541ft/1078m

Strong mountain

Distance_____ Miles/Km   Height_____ ft/m   Date____/____/____

Weather      _____

Companions   _____

Route        _____

and Notes    _____

_____

_____

_____

_____

_____

_____

_____

_____


## Glas Bheinn Mhor                                     3258ft/993m

Big, grey mountain

Distance_____ Miles/Km   Height_____ ft/m   Date____/____/____

Weather      _____

Companions   _____

Route        _____

and Notes    _____

_____

_____

_____

_____

_____

_____

_____

_____

| Beinn nan Aighenan | 3141ft/957m |
|---|---|

Mountain of the hinds

Distance_____ Miles/Km   Height_____ ft/m   Date___/___/___

Weather _____

Companions _____

Route _____

and Notes _____

_____

_____

_____

_____

_____

_____

_____


| Stob Coir'an Albannaich | 3425ft/1044m |
|---|---|

Peak of the corrie of the Scotsman

Distance_____ Miles/Km   Height_____ ft/m   Date___/___/___

Weather _____

Companions _____

Route _____

and Notes _____

_____

_____

_____

_____

_____

_____

_____

## Meall nan Eun                                3039ft/926m

Hill of the birds

Distance_____ Miles/Km   Height_____ ft/m   Date____/____/____

Weather      _____

Companions   _____

Route        _____

and Notes    _____

_____

_____

_____

_____

_____

_____

_____

_____


## Stob Ghabhar                                3565ft/1087m

Peak of the goats

Distance_____ Miles/Km   Height_____ ft/m   Date____/____/____

Weather      _____

Companions   _____

Route        _____

and Notes    _____

_____

_____

_____

_____

_____

_____

_____

_____

## Stob a'Choire Odhair                                    3058ft/947m
Peak of the dun corrie

Distance_____ Miles/Km   Height_____ ft/m   Date____/____/____

Weather        _____

Companions     _____

Route          _____

and Notes      _____

_____

_____

_____

_____

_____

_____

_____

_____


## Creise                                              3608ft/1100m★
Origin unknown

Distance_____ Miles/Km   Height_____ ft/m   Date____/____/____

Weather        _____

Companions     _____

Route          _____

and Notes      _____

_____

_____

_____

_____

_____

_____

_____

★ Prior to map revisions Munro's list pre-1980, Clach Leathad was given as the highest point, and therefore of mountain status.

## Meall a'Bhuiridh                                3636ft/1108m

Hill of the roaring

Distance_____ Miles/Km    Height_____ ft/m    Date____/____/____

Weather _____

Companions _____

Route _____

and Notes _____

_____

_____

_____

_____

_____

_____

_____

## Buachaille Etive Mor – Stob Dearg                  3345ft/1022m

The big herdsman of Etive – Red Peak

Distance_____ Miles/Km    Height_____ ft/m    Date____/____/____

Weather _____

Companions _____

Route _____

and Notes _____

_____

_____

_____

_____

_____

_____

_____

## Buachaille Etive Beag – Stob Dubh                    3129ft/958m

The little herdsman of Etive – Black peak

Distance_____ Miles/Km   Height_____ ft/m   Date____/____/____

Weather      _____

Companions   _____

Route        _____

and Notes    _____

_____

_____

_____

_____

_____

_____

_____


## Bidean nam Bian                                      3766ft/1150m

Pinnacle of the hides

Distance_____ Miles/Km   Height_____ ft/m   Date____/____/____

Weather      _____

Companions   _____

Route        _____

and Notes    _____

_____

_____

_____

_____

_____

_____

_____

## Sgor na h-Ulaidh       3258ft/994m

Peak of the hidden treasure

Distance_____ Miles/Km   Height_____ ft/m   Date___/___/___

Weather    _____

Companions   _____

Route      _____

and Notes    _____

_____

_____

_____

_____

_____

_____

_____

_____


## Beinn Fhionnlaidh       3145ft/959m

Finlay's mountain

Distance_____ Miles/Km   Height_____ ft/m   Date___/___/___

Weather    _____

Companions   _____

Route      _____

and Notes    _____

_____

_____

_____

_____

_____

_____

_____

_____

## Beinn Sgulaird 3059ft/932m

Origin unknown

Distance_____ Miles/Km   Height_____ ft/m   Date____/____/____

Weather      _____

Companions   _____

Route        _____

and Notes    _____

_____

_____

_____

_____

_____

_____

_____

## Beinn a'Bheithir – Sgorr Dhearg 3361ft/1024m

Mountain of the monster – Red peak

Distance_____ Miles/Km   Height_____ ft/m   Date____/____/____

Weather      _____

Companions   _____

Route        _____

and Notes    _____

_____

_____

_____

_____

_____

_____

_____

49

## Beinn a'Bheithir – Sgorr Dhonuill                3284ft/1001m

Mountain of the monster – Donald's peak

Distance_____ Miles/Km   Height_____ ft/m   Date____/____/____

Weather     _____

Companions  _____

Route       _____

and Notes   _____

_____

_____

_____

_____

_____

_____

_____

_____

_____

# 5 North Glencoe, Nether Lochaber, Alder and West Drumochter

*Stob Coire a'Chairn and Sgurr a'Mhaim*

| Aonach Eagach – Sgorr nam Fiannaidh | 3173ft/967m |
|---|---|

Notched ridge – Peak of the Fianns

Distance_____ Miles/Km   Height_____ ft/m   Date____/____/____

Weather   _____

Companions _____

Route   _____

and Notes   _____

_____

_____

_____

_____

_____

_____

_____


| Aonach Eagach – Meall Dearg | 3118ft/951m |
|---|---|

Notched ridge – Red hill

Distance_____ Miles/Km   Height_____ ft/m   Date____/____/____

Weather   _____

Companions _____

Route   _____

and Notes   _____

_____

_____

_____

_____

_____

_____

_____

52

## Sgurr Eilde Mor                                            3279ft/1008m

Big crag of the hinds

Distance_____ Miles/Km   Height_____ ft/m   Date____/____/____

Weather     _____

Companions  _____

Route       _____

and Notes   _____

_____

_____

_____

_____

_____

_____

_____

## Binnein Beag                                               3083ft/940m

Little hill

Distance_____ Miles/Km   Height_____ ft/m   Date____/____/____

Weather     _____

Companions  _____

Route       _____

and Notes   _____

_____

_____

_____

_____

_____

_____

_____

| **Binnein Mor** | | | | **3700ft/1128m** |
| --- | --- | --- | --- | --- |

Big hill

Distance_____ Miles/Km   Height_____ ft/m   Date____/____/____

Weather _____

Companions _____

Route _____

and Notes _____

_____

_____

_____

_____

_____

_____

_____

_____


| **Na Gruagaichean** | | | | **3442ft/1055m** |
| --- | --- | --- | --- | --- |

The maidens

Distance_____ Miles/Km   Height_____ ft/m   Date____/____/____

Weather _____

Companions _____

Route _____

and Notes _____

_____

_____

_____

_____

_____

_____

_____

## An Gearanach                                          3230ft/985m
The short ridge

Distance_____ Miles/Km   Height_____ ft/m   Date___/___/___

Weather      _____

Companions   _____

Route        _____

and Notes    _____

_____

_____

_____

_____

_____

_____

_____

_____


## Stob Coire a'Chairn                                   3219ft/983m
Peak of the corrie of the cairn

Distance_____ Miles/Km   Height_____ ft/m   Date___/___/___

Weather      _____

Companions   _____

Route        _____

and Notes    _____

_____

_____

_____

_____

_____

_____

_____

| **Am Bodach** | **3382ft/1034m** |

The old man

Distance_____ Miles/Km   Height_____ ft/m   Date___/___/___

Weather _____

Companions _____

Route _____

and Notes _____

_____

_____

_____

_____

_____

_____

_____

_____

| **Sgurr a'Mhaim** | **3601ft/1098m** |

Peak of the large, rounded hill

Distance_____ Miles/Km   Height_____ ft/m   Date___/___/___

Weather _____

Companions _____

Route _____

and Notes _____

_____

_____

_____

_____

_____

_____

_____

_____

## Sgor an Iubhair ‡          3284ft/1001m
Peak of the yew tree

Distance_____ Miles/Km   Height_____ ft/m   Date___/___/___

Weather _____

Companions _____

Route _____

and Notes _____

_____

_____

_____

_____

_____

_____

_____

_____


## Stob Ban          3274ft/999m
White peak

Distance_____ Miles/Km   Height_____ ft/m   Date___/___/___

Weather _____

Companions _____

Route _____

and Notes _____

_____

_____

_____

_____

_____

_____

_____

_____

57

‡ Demoted to Top in the *Munro's Tables* of 1997.

| **Mullach nan Coirean** | **3077ft/939m** |

Top of the corries

Distance_____ Miles/Km   Height_____ ft/m   Date____/____/____

Weather _____

Companions _____

Route _____

and Notes _____

_____

_____

_____

_____

_____

_____

_____

_____

| **Ben Nevis** | **4406ft/1344m** |

Venomous or malicious mountain, or mountain with its head in the clouds

Distance_____ Miles/Km   Height_____ ft/m   Date____/____/____

Weather _____

Companions _____

Route _____

and Notes _____

_____

_____

_____

_____

_____

_____

_____

## Carn Mor Dearg 4012ft/1223m

Big red cairn

Distance_____ Miles/Km   Height_____ ft/m   Date___/___/___

Weather _____

Companions _____

Route _____

and Notes _____

_____

_____

_____

_____

_____

_____

_____


## Aonach Mor 3999ft/1219m

Great ridge

Distance_____ Miles/Km   Height_____ ft/m   Date___/___/___

Weather _____

Companions _____

Route _____

and Notes _____

_____

_____

_____

_____

_____

_____

_____

## Aonach Beag                                                    4060ft/1236m
Little ridge

Distance_____ Miles/Km   Height_____ ft/m   Date___/___/___

Weather       _____

Companions  _____

Route         _____

and Notes    _____

_____

_____

_____

_____

_____

_____

_____

_____


## Sgurr Choinnich Mor                                            3603ft/1095m
The big, mossy peak

Distance_____ Miles/Km   Height_____ ft/m   Date___/___/___

Weather       _____

Companions  _____

Route         _____

and Notes    _____

_____

_____

_____

_____

_____

_____

_____

_____

## Stob Coire an Laoigh — 3657ft/1115m

Peak of the corrie of the calf

Distance_____ Miles/Km   Height_____ ft/m   Date____/____/____

Weather      _____

Companions   _____

Route        _____

and Notes    _____

_____

_____

_____

_____

_____

_____

_____

## Stob Choire Claurigh — 3858ft/1177m

Peak of the brawling corrie

Distance_____ Miles/Km   Height_____ ft/m   Date____/____/____

Weather      _____

Companions   _____

Route        _____

and Notes    _____

_____

_____

_____

_____

_____

_____

_____

## Stob Ban                                                    3217ft/977m
White peak

Distance_____ Miles/Km   Height_____ ft/m   Date____/____/____

Weather _____

Companions _____

Route _____

and Notes _____

_____

_____

_____

_____

_____

_____

_____


## Stob Coire Easain                                          3658ft/1116m
Peak of the corrie of the waterfalls

Distance_____ Miles/Km   Height_____ ft/m   Date____/____/____

Weather _____

Companions _____

Route _____

and Notes _____

_____

_____

_____

_____

_____

_____

_____

## Stob a'Choire Mheadhoin            3610ft/1106m
Peak of the middle corrie

Distance_____ Miles/Km   Height_____ ft/m   Date\_\_\_\_/\_\_\_\_/\_\_\_\_

Weather

Companions

Route

and Notes

## Stob Coire Sgriodain            3211ft/976m
Peak of the scree corrie

Distance_____ Miles/Km   Height_____ ft/m   Date\_\_\_\_/\_\_\_\_/\_\_\_\_

Weather

Companions

Route

and Notes

| Chno Dearg | 3433ft/1047m |
|---|---|

Red nut

Distance_____ Miles/Km  Height_____ ft/m  Date\_\_\_\_/\_\_\_\_/\_\_\_\_

Weather _____

Companions _____

Route _____

and Notes _____

| Beinn na Lap | 3066ft/937m |
|---|---|

Boggy mountain

Distance_____ Miles/Km  Height_____ ft/m  Date\_\_\_\_/\_\_\_\_/\_\_\_\_

Weather _____

Companions _____

Route _____

and Notes _____

## Carn Dearg                                     3080ft/941m
Red cairn

Distance_____ Miles/Km   Height_____ ft/m   Date___/___/___
Weather       _____
Companions    _____
Route         _____
and Notes     _____

_____
_____
_____
_____
_____
_____
_____
_____

## Sgor Gaibhre                                   3124ft/955m
Peak of the goats

Distance_____ Miles/Km   Height_____ ft/m   Date___/___/___
Weather       _____
Companions    _____
Route         _____
and Notes     _____

_____
_____
_____
_____
_____
_____
_____
_____

## Beinn Eibhinn                    3611ft/1100m

Mountain of the fair outlook, or delightful mountain

Distance_____ Miles/Km   Height_____ ft/m   Date___/___/___

Weather      _____

Companions   _____

Route        _____

and Notes    _____

_____

_____

_____

_____

_____

_____

_____

_____


## Aonach Beag                      3647ft/1114m

Little ridge

Distance_____ Miles/Km   Height_____ ft/m   Date___/___/___

Weather      _____

Companions   _____

Route        _____

and Notes    _____

_____

_____

_____

_____

_____

_____

_____

## Geal Charn                                            3656ft/1132m

White cairn

Distance_____ Miles/Km   Height_____ ft/m   Date\_\_\_\_/\_\_\_\_/\_\_\_\_

Weather

Companions

Route

and Notes

---

## Carn Dearg                                           3391ft/1034m

Red cairn

Distance_____ Miles/Km   Height_____ ft/m   Date\_\_\_\_/\_\_\_\_/\_\_\_\_

Weather

Companions

Route

and Notes

## Beinn a'Chlachair                    3569ft/1088m

Mason's mountain

Distance_____ Miles/Km   Height_____ ft/m   Date____/____/____

Weather _____

Companions _____

Route _____

and Notes _____

_____

_____

_____

_____

_____

_____


## Mullach Coire an Iubhair            3443ft/1049m★

Top of the corrie of the yew tree

Distance_____ Miles/Km   Height_____ ft/m   Date____/____/____

Weather _____

Companions _____

Route _____

and Notes _____

_____

_____

_____

_____

_____

★ O.S. 1:50 000 map gives Geal Charn – White Cairn.

68

## Creag Pitridh                                     3031ft/924m
Rock of the hollow places, or Petrie's Crag

Distance_____ Miles/Km   Height_____ ft/m   Date\_\_\_/\_\_\_/\_\_\_

Weather _____

Companions _____

Route _____

and Notes _____

_____

_____

_____

_____

_____

_____

_____

## Ben Alder                                          3765ft/1148m
Mountain of rock and water

Distance_____ Miles/Km   Height_____ ft/m   Date\_\_\_/\_\_\_/\_\_\_

Weather _____

Companions _____

Route _____

and Notes _____

_____

_____

_____

_____

_____

_____

_____

| **Beinn Bheoil** | **3333ft/1019m** |

Mountain in front (of Ben Alder)

Distance_____ Miles/Km   Height_____ ft/m   Date___/___/___

Weather _____

Companions _____

Route _____

and Notes _____

_____

_____

_____

_____

_____

_____

_____

_____

_____

| **Sgairneach Mhor** | **3251ft/991m** |

Big rocky hillside

Distance_____ Miles/Km   Height_____ ft/m   Date___/___/___

Weather _____

Companions _____

Route _____

and Notes _____

_____

_____

_____

_____

_____

_____

_____

_____

| Beinn Udlamain | 3306ft/1010m |
|---|---|

Mountain of the unsteady place

Distance_____ Miles/Km  Height_____ ft/m  Date____/____/____

Weather  _____

Companions  _____

Route  _____

and Notes  _____

_____

_____

_____

_____

_____

_____

_____

| A'Mharconaich | 3185ft/975m |
|---|---|

The horse place

Distance_____ Miles/Km  Height_____ ft/m  Date____/____/____

Weather  _____

Companions  _____

Route  _____

and Notes  _____

_____

_____

_____

_____

_____

_____

_____

71

## Geal-charn                                          3005ft/917m

White cairn

Distance_____ Miles/Km   Height_____ ft/m   Date\_\_\_/\_\_\_/\_\_\_

Weather   _____

Companions  _____

Route    _____

and Notes  _____

# 6 Loch Laggan and the Monadh Liath

*Beinn a'Chaorainn*

## Beinn Teallach                                        2994ft/915m★
### Forge mountain

Distance_____ Miles/Km   Height_____ ft/m   Date___/___/___

Weather _____

Companions _____

Route _____

and Notes _____

_____

_____

_____

_____

_____

_____

_____


## Beinn a'Chaorainn                                     3453ft/1052m
### Mountain of the rowan tree

Distance_____ Miles/Km   Height_____ ft/m   Date___/___/___

Weather _____

Companions _____

Route _____

and Notes _____

_____

_____

_____

_____

_____

_____

★ Recognised as over 3000ft from O.S. 1:25 000 map – entered to revised Munro's list in 1990.

74

## Creag Meagaidh                                  3700ft/1130m
### Bogland rock

Distance_____ Miles/Km   Height_____ ft/m   Date____/____/____

Weather     _____

Companions  _____

Route       _____

and Notes   _____

_____

_____

_____

_____

_____

_____

_____


## Stob Poite Coire Ardair                          3460ft/1053m
### Pot of the high corrie

Distance_____ Miles/Km   Height_____ ft/m   Date____/____/____

Weather     _____

Companions  _____

Route       _____

and Notes   _____

_____

_____

_____

_____

_____

_____

_____

| Carn Liath | 3298ft/1006m |

Grey hill

Distance_____ Miles/Km   Height_____ ft/m   Date___/___/___

Weather _____

Companions _____

Route _____

and Notes _____

_____

_____

_____

_____

_____

_____

_____

| Carn Dearg | 3093ft/945m |

Red cairn

Distance_____ Miles/Km   Height_____ ft/m   Date___/___/___

Weather _____

Companions _____

Route _____

and Notes _____

_____

_____

_____

_____

_____

_____

_____

## Carn Ban                                    3087ft/942m★

White cairn

Distance_____ Miles/Km   Height_____ ft/m   Date___/___/___

Weather        _____

Companions     _____

Route          _____

and Notes      _____

_____

_____

_____

_____

_____

_____

_____


## Carn Ballach                                3020ft/920m★

Cairn of the pass

Distance_____ Miles/Km   Height_____ ft/m   Date___/___/___

Weather        _____

Companions     _____

Route          _____

and Notes      _____

_____

_____

_____

_____

_____

★ Deleted from Munro's list in 1980.

## Carn Sgulain                                      3015ft/920m

Cairn of the basket

Distance_____ Miles/Km   Height_____ ft/m   Date___/___/___

Weather      _____

Companions   _____

Route        _____

and Notes    _____

_____

_____

_____

_____

_____

_____

_____


## A'Chailleach                                      3054ft/930m

The old woman

Distance_____ Miles/Km   Height_____ ft/m   Date___/___/___

Weather      _____

Companions   _____

Route        _____

and Notes    _____

_____

_____

_____

_____

_____

_____

## Geal Charn 3036ft/926m

White cairn

Distance_____ Miles/Km  Height_____ ft/m  Date____/____/____

Weather _____

Companions _____

Route _____

and Notes _____

_____

_____

_____

_____

_____

_____

_____

_____

# 7   Lochy, Arkaig, Knoydart, Quoich and South Glen Shiel

*Sgurr na Ciche and Garbh Chioch Mhor*

## Sron a'Choire Ghairbh 3066ft/935m

The nose of the rough corrie

Distance_____ Miles/Km  Height_____ ft/m  Date___/___/___

Weather _____

Companions _____

Route _____

and Notes _____

_____

_____

_____

_____

_____

_____

_____

## Meall na Teanga 3010ft/917m

The lump of the tongue

Distance_____ Miles/Km  Height_____ ft/m  Date___/___/___

Weather _____

Companions _____

Route _____

and Notes _____

_____

_____

_____

_____

_____

_____

_____

## Gaor Bheinn (Gulvain)                                    3224ft/987m

Thrill, or filthy mountain

Distance_____ Miles/Km   Height_____ ft/m   Date___/___/___

Weather       _____

Companions   _____

Route         _____

and Notes     _____

_____

_____

_____

_____

_____

_____

_____

_____


## Sgurr Thuilm                                             3164ft/963m

The peak of the holm

Distance_____ Miles/Km   Height_____ ft/m   Date___/___/___

Weather       _____

Companions   _____

Route         _____

and Notes     _____

_____

_____

_____

_____

_____

_____

_____

## Sgurr nan Coireachan                                         3136ft/956m

The peak of the corries

Distance_____ Miles/Km   Height_____ ft/m   Date____/____/____

Weather          _____

Companions       _____

Route            _____

and Notes        _____

_____

_____

_____

_____

_____

_____

_____


## Sgurr na Ciche                                              3410ft/1040m

The pap shaped peak

Distance_____ Miles/Km   Height_____ ft/m   Date____/____/____

Weather          _____

Companions       _____

Route            _____

and Notes        _____

_____

_____

_____

_____

_____

_____

_____

## Garbh Chioch Mhor                    3365ft/1013m*

*The big, rough pap*

Distance_____ Miles/Km  Height_____ ft/m  Date____/____/____

Weather         _____

Companions      _____

Route           _____

and Notes       _____

_____

_____

_____

_____

_____

_____

_____

_____

## Sgurr nan Coireachan                 3125ft/953m

*The peak of the corries*

Distance_____ Miles/Km  Height_____ ft/m  Date____/____/____

Weather         _____

Companions      _____

Route           _____

and Notes       _____

_____

_____

_____

_____

_____

_____

_____

* Entered to Munro's list 1980.

## Sgurr Mor                                                3290ft/1003m

The great peak

Distance_____ Miles/Km   Height_____ ft/m   Date____/____/____

Weather      _____

Companions   _____

Route        _____

and Notes    _____

_____

_____

_____

_____

_____

_____

_____


## Gairich                                                  3015ft/919m

The peak of yelling

Distance_____ Miles/Km   Height_____ ft/m   Date____/____/____

Weather      _____

Companions   _____

Route        _____

and Notes    _____

_____

_____

_____

_____

_____

_____

_____

## Meall Buidhe                                              3107ft/946m
### The yellow lump

Distance_____ Miles/Km   Height_____ ft/m   Date____/____/____

Weather _____

Companions _____

Route _____

and Notes _____

_____

_____

_____

_____

_____

_____

_____

_____


## Luinne Bheinn                                            3083ft/939m
### Hill of anger, mirth or melody

Distance_____ Miles/Km   Height_____ ft/m   Date____/____/____

Weather _____

Companions _____

Route _____

and Notes _____

_____

_____

_____

_____

_____

_____

_____

## Ladhar Bheinn 3343ft/1020m

The forked mountain

Distance_____ Miles/Km  Height_____ ft/m  Date____/____/____

Weather _____

Companions _____

Route _____

and Notes _____

_____

_____

_____

_____

_____

_____

_____

## Beinn Sgritheall (Ben Sgriol) 3196ft/974m

Scree or gravel hill

Distance_____ Miles/Km  Height_____ ft/m  Date____/____/____

Weather _____

Companions _____

Route _____

and Notes _____

_____

_____

_____

_____

_____

_____

## The Saddle       3317ft/1010m

Name taken from the mountain's profile

Distance_____ Miles/Km   Height_____ ft/m   Date____/____/____

Weather _____

Companions _____

Route _____

and Notes _____

_____

_____

_____

_____

_____

_____

_____

_____


## Sgurr na Sgine       3098ft/945m

The peak of the knife

Distance_____ Miles/Km   Height_____ ft/m   Date____/____/____

Weather _____

Companions _____

Route _____

and Notes _____

_____

_____

_____

_____

_____

_____

_____

## Sgurr a'Mhaoraich 3365ft/1027m

The peak of the shell fish

Distance_____ Miles/Km  Height_____ ft/m  Date____/____/____

Weather  _____

Companions  _____

Route  _____

and Notes  _____

_____

_____

_____

_____

_____

_____

_____

_____

## Gleouraich 3395ft/1035m

Uproar

Distance_____ Miles/Km  Height_____ ft/m  Date____/____/____

Weather  _____

Companions  _____

Route  _____

and Notes  _____

_____

_____

_____

_____

_____

_____

_____

_____

| Spidean Mialach | 3268ft/996m |

The pinnacle of the wild animals

Distance_____ Miles/Km   Height_____ ft/m   Date___/___/___

Weather _____

Companions _____

Route _____

and Notes _____

_____

_____

_____

_____

_____

_____

_____

_____


| Creag a'Mhaim | 3102ft/947m |

Crag of the large, rounded hill

Distance_____ Miles/Km   Height_____ ft/m   Date___/___/___

Weather _____

Companions _____

Route _____

and Notes _____

_____

_____

_____

_____

_____

_____

_____

## Druim Shionnach      3222ft/987m

The ridge of the foxes

Distance_____ Miles/Km   Height_____ ft/m   Date____/____/____

Weather     _____

Companions     _____

Route     _____

and Notes     _____

_____

_____

_____

_____

_____

_____

_____

_____


## Aonach air Chrith      3342ft/1021m

The shaking height

Distance_____ Miles/Km   Height_____ ft/m   Date____/____/____

Weather     _____

Companions     _____

Route     _____

and Notes     _____

_____

_____

_____

_____

_____

_____

_____

## Maol Chinn-dearg                                        3214ft/981m

The bald, redheaded hill

Distance_____ Miles/Km   Height_____ ft/m   Date___/___/___

Weather _____

Companions _____

Route _____

and Notes _____

_____

_____

_____

_____

_____

_____

_____

_____

## Sgurr an Doire Leathain                                 3272ft/1010m

The peak of the broad thicket

Distance_____ Miles/Km   Height_____ ft/m   Date___/___/___

Weather _____

Companions _____

Route _____

and Notes _____

_____

_____

_____

_____

_____

_____

_____

_____

## Sgurr an Lochain 3282ft/1004m
The peak of the little loch

Distance_____ Miles/Km  Height_____ ft/m  Date____/____/____

Weather

Companions

Route

and Notes

## Creag nan Damh 3012ft/918m
The rock of the stag

Distance_____ Miles/Km  Height_____ ft/m  Date____/____/____

Weather

Companions

Route

and Notes

# 8   Kintail, Ceannacroc and Affric

*The South Cluanie Ridge*

## Sgurr Fhuaran                                    3505ft/1068m

Peak of the well

Distance_____ Miles/Km   Height_____ ft/m   Date____/____/____

Weather       _____

Companions    _____

Route         _____

and Notes     _____

_____

_____

_____

_____

_____

_____

_____

_____


## Sgurr na Ciste Duibhe                            3370ft/1027m

The peak of the black chest

Distance_____ Miles/Km   Height_____ ft/m   Date____/____/____

Weather       _____

Companions    _____

Route         _____

and Notes     _____

_____

_____

_____

_____

_____

_____

_____

_____

## Saileag                                                         3124ft/959m

The little heel

Distance_____ Miles/Km   Height_____ ft/m   Date____/____/____

Weather         _____

Companions   _____

Route            _____

and Notes     _____

_____

_____

_____

_____

_____

_____

_____


## Sgurr a'Bhealaich Dheirg                                       3378ft/1031m

The peak of the red gap

Distance_____ Miles/Km   Height_____ ft/m   Date____/____/____

Weather         _____

Companions   _____

Route            _____

and Notes     _____

_____

_____

_____

_____

_____

_____

_____

## Aonach Meadhoin 3284ft/1003m

Middle ridge

Distance_____ Miles/Km  Height_____ ft/m  Date____/____/____

Weather _____

Companions _____

Route _____

and Notes _____

_____

_____

_____

_____

_____

_____

_____


## Ciste Dhubh 3218ft/982m

The black chest

Distance_____ Miles/Km  Height_____ ft/m  Date____/____/____

Weather _____

Companions _____

Route _____

and Notes _____

_____

_____

_____

_____

_____

_____

_____

## Mullach Fraoch-choire                           3614ft/1102m

The top of the heather corrie

Distance_____ Miles/Km   Height_____ ft/m   Date____/____/____

Weather _____

Companions _____

Route _____

and Notes _____

_____

_____

_____

_____

_____

_____

_____

_____


## A'Chralaig                                      3673ft/1120m

The basket or creel

Distance_____ Miles/Km   Height_____ ft/m   Date____/____/____

Weather _____

Companions _____

Route _____

and Notes _____

_____

_____

_____

_____

_____

_____

_____

| **Tigh Mor na Seilge** | **3285ft/1002m★** |

The big house of hunting

Distance_____ Miles/Km  Height_____ ft/m  Date\_\_\_/\_\_\_/\_\_\_

Weather _____

Companions _____

Route _____

and Notes _____

| **Sgurr nan Conbhairean** | **3635ft/1109m** |

The peak of the dog men

Distance_____ Miles/Km  Height_____ ft/m  Date\_\_\_/\_\_\_/\_\_\_

Weather _____

Companions _____

Route _____

and Notes _____

★ Also known as Sail Chaorainn – Heel of the rowan tree.

## Carn Ghluasaid                                          3140ft/957m

The cairn of moving

Distance_____ Miles/Km   Height_____ ft/m   Date____/____/____

Weather     _____

Companions  _____

Route       _____

and Notes   _____

            _____

            _____

            _____

            _____

            _____

            _____

            _____

            _____


## A'Ghlas-bheinn                                          3006ft/918m

The green mountain

Distance_____ Miles/Km   Height_____ ft/m   Date____/____/____

Weather     _____

Companions  _____

Route       _____

and Notes   _____

            _____

            _____

            _____

            _____

            _____

            _____

            _____

100

## Beinn Fhada (Ben Attow)                    3385ft/1032m
The long mountain

Distance_____ Miles/Km   Height_____ ft/m   Date\_\_\_/\_\_\_/\_\_\_

Weather          _____

Companions       _____

Route            _____

and Notes        _____

## Sgurr nan Ceathreamhnan                    3771ft/1151m
The peak of the quarters

Distance_____ Miles/Km   Height_____ ft/m   Date\_\_\_/\_\_\_/\_\_\_

Weather          _____

Companions       _____

Route            _____

and Notes        _____

101

| Creag a'choir Aird | 3210ft/982m* |

The rock of the high corrie

Distance_____ Miles/Km   Height_____ ft/m   Date\_\_\_/\_\_\_/\_\_\_

Weather _____

Companions _____

Route _____

and Notes _____

| An Socach | 3017ft/920m |

The snout

Distance_____ Miles/Km   Height_____ ft/m   Date\_\_\_/\_\_\_/\_\_\_

Weather _____

Companions _____

Route _____

and Notes _____

* Also known as Mullach na Dheiragain – The redder, round hill.

102

## Mam Sodhail (Mam Soul)                    3862ft/1181m

The round hill of the barns

Distance_____ Miles/Km   Height_____ ft/m   Date___/___/___

Weather _____

Companions _____

Route _____

and Notes _____

_____

_____

_____

_____

_____

_____

_____


## Carn Eige (Eighe)                         3880ft/1183m

Cairn of the notch or file

Distance_____ Miles/Km   Height_____ ft/m   Date___/___/___

Weather _____

Companions _____

Route _____

and Notes _____

_____

_____

_____

_____

_____

_____

_____

_____

## Beinn Fhionnlaidh | 3294ft/1005m

Finlay's mountain

Distance_____ Miles/Km   Height_____ ft/m   Date___/___/___

Weather _____

Companions _____

Route _____

and Notes _____

_____

_____

_____

_____

_____

_____

_____

## Tom a'Choinich | 3646ft/1111m

The mossy hillock

Distance_____ Miles/Km   Height_____ ft/m   Date___/___/___

Weather _____

Companions _____

Route _____

and Notes _____

_____

_____

_____

_____

_____

_____

_____

## Toll Creagach 3455ft/1053m

The rocky hole

Distance_____ Miles/Km  Height_____ ft/m  Date____/____/____

Weather _____

Companions _____

Route _____

and Notes _____

_____

_____

_____

_____

_____

_____

_____

_____

# 9    Cannich, Strathfarrar,
## Monar and Glen Carron

*Bidein a'Choire Sheasgaich*

## Carn nan Gobhar                                    3251ft/992m

Cairn of the goats

Distance_____ Miles/Km   Height_____ ft/m   Date____/____/____

Weather     _____

Companions  _____

Route       _____

and Notes   _____

_____

_____

_____

_____

_____

_____

_____

_____


## Sgurr na Lapaich                                   3775ft/1150m

The peak of the bog

Distance_____ Miles/Km   Height_____ ft/m   Date____/____/____

Weather     _____

Companions  _____

Route       _____

and Notes   _____

_____

_____

_____

_____

_____

_____

_____

_____

## An Riabhachan                                           3696ft/1129m

The brindled hill

Distance_____ Miles/Km   Height_____ ft/m   Date____/____/____

Weather     _____

Companions  _____

Route       _____

and Notes   _____

_____

_____

_____

_____

_____

_____

_____

## An Socach                                              3508ft/1069m

The snout

Distance_____ Miles/Km   Height_____ ft/m   Date____/____/____

Weather     _____

Companions  _____

Route       _____

and Notes   _____

_____

_____

_____

_____

_____

_____

_____

## Sgurr na Ruaidhe                                          3254ft/993m
The peak of the red hind

Distance_____ Miles/Km  Height_____ ft/m  Date____/____/____

Weather        _____

Companions     _____

Route          _____

and Notes      _____

_____

_____

_____

_____

_____

_____

_____


## Carn nan Gobhar                                           3251ft/992m
Cairn of the goats

Distance_____ Miles/Km  Height_____ ft/m  Date____/____/____

Weather        _____

Companions     _____

Route          _____

and Notes      _____

_____

_____

_____

_____

_____

_____

_____

## Sgurr a'Choire Ghlais                                    3554ft/1083m

The peak of the green corrie

Distance_____ Miles/Km   Height_____ ft/m   Date____/____/____

Weather      _____

Companions   _____

Route        _____

and Notes    _____

_____

_____

_____

_____

_____

_____

_____


## Sgurr Fhuar-thuill                                      3439ft/1049m

The peak of the cold hole

Distance_____ Miles/Km   Height_____ ft/m   Date____/____/____

Weather      _____

Companions   _____

Route        _____

and Notes    _____

_____

_____

_____

_____

_____

_____

_____

110

## Maoile Lunndaidh        3304ft/1007m*

The hill of the boggy place

Distance_____ Miles/Km   Height_____ ft/m   Date____/____/____

Weather   _____

Companions  _____

Route     _____

and Notes   _____

_____

_____

_____

_____

_____

_____

_____

## Sgurr a' Chaorachain        3455ft/1053m

The peak of the white, boiling, tumbling torrent

Distance_____ Miles/Km   Height_____ ft/m   Date____/____/____

Weather   _____

Companions  _____

Route     _____

and Notes   _____

_____

_____

_____

_____

_____

_____

* Prior to map revisions, Munro's list pre-1974, Creag Toll a'Choin was given as the highest point, and therefore of mountain status.

| **Sgurr Choinnich** | **3276ft/999m** |

Mossy peak

Distance_____ Miles/Km   Height_____ ft/m   Date____/____/____

Weather   _____

Companions   _____

Route   _____

and Notes   _____

_____

_____

_____

_____

_____

_____

_____

_____

| **Bidein a'Choire Sheasgaich** | **3102ft/945m** |

The little peak of the reedy corrie

Distance_____ Miles/Km   Height_____ ft/m   Date____/____/____

Weather   _____

Companions   _____

Route   _____

and Notes   _____

_____

_____

_____

_____

_____

_____

_____

_____

*Sgiath Chuil from Glen Dochart*                    *I Butterfield*

*Ben Starav from Inbhirfhaolain*                                              *R Gibbens*

*Ben Nevis from Carn Mor Dearg*                                        *G Blyth*

*Beinn a'Chlachair and Loch Pattack*                                        *I Butterfield*

*Coire Ardair of Creag Meagaidh*                                                     *J Teesdale*

*Ladhar Bheinn*                                                    *R Wood*

*Sgurr na Lapaich*                                                    *D J Bennet*

*Sgurr na Lapaich*

*D J Bennet*

*Beinn Eighe from Cromasaig*                                        *I Butterfield*

*Seana Bhraigh and Luchd Choire*                                            *D J Bennet*

*Cairn Toul from Braeriach*                                        *R Everett*

*Broad Cairn and Loch Muick*                                            *I Brown*

*Sgurr Mhic Choinnich and Sgurr Dubh Mor from the Inaccessible Pinnacle*    N Williams

*Helvellyn and Striding Edge*                    *P Hodgkiss*

*Tryfan from Glyder Fach*                                                        *R Gibbens*

*Macgillycuddy's Reeks from Upper Lake*                                    *I Butterfield*

## Lurg Mhor       3234ft/986m

The big shank

Distance_____ Miles/Km   Height_____ ft/m   Date____/____/____

Weather

Companions

Route

and Notes

## Moruisg       3026ft/928m

Big water

Distance_____ Miles/Km   Height_____ ft/m   Date____/____/____

Weather

Companions

Route

and Notes

## Sgurr nan Ceannaichean | 2896ft/915m★

The peak of the merchants

Distance_____ Miles/Km   Height_____ ft/m   Date___/___/___

Weather _____

Companions _____

Route _____

and Notes _____

_____

_____

_____

_____

_____

_____

_____

_____

★ Recognised as over 3000ft from O.S. 1:50 000 map – entered to revised Munro's list in 1980.

# 10　The Torridons

*Beinn Alligin*

## Beinn Liath Mhor                                         3034ft/925m
The big grey mountain

Distance_____ Miles/Km   Height_____ ft/m   Date___/___/___

Weather        _____

Companions     _____

Route          _____

and Notes      _____

_____

_____

_____

_____

_____

_____

_____


## Sgorr Ruadh                                              3142ft/960m
The red peak

Distance_____ Miles/Km   Height_____ ft/m   Date___/___/___

Weather        _____

Companions     _____

Route          _____

and Notes      _____

_____

_____

_____

_____

_____

_____

_____

## Maol Chean-dearg           3060ft/933m

The bald, red head

Distance_____ Miles/Km   Height_____ ft/m   Date____/____/____

Weather       _____

Companions   _____

Route         _____

and Notes     _____

_____

_____

_____

_____

_____

_____

_____

_____

## Beinn Alligin (Sgurr Mhor)        3232ft/985m

The mountain of beauty or jewel mountain (Big peak)

Distance_____ Miles/Km   Height_____ ft/m   Date____/____/____

Weather       _____

Companions   _____

Route         _____

and Notes     _____

_____

_____

_____

_____

_____

_____

_____

## Liathach – Spidean a'Choire Leith                 3456ft/1054m
### The grey one – The peak of the grey corrie

Distance_____ Miles/Km   Height_____ ft/m   Date____/____/____

Weather _____

Companions _____

Route _____

and Notes _____

_____

_____

_____

_____

_____

_____

_____

_____

## Liathach – Mullach an Rathain                      3358ft/1023m★
### The grey one – The top above the horns

Distance_____ Miles/Km   Height_____ ft/m   Date____/____/____

Weather _____

Companions _____

Route _____

and Notes _____

_____

_____

_____

_____

_____

_____

★ Entered to revised Munro's list 1980.

118

## Beinn Eighe – Ruadh-stac Mor          **3309ft/1010m**

The mountain of ice or the mountain of the file – Big red peak

Distance_____ Miles/Km   Height_____ ft/m   Date____/____/____

Weather         _____

Companions   _____

Route            _____

and Notes      _____

_____

_____

_____

_____

_____

_____

_____

_____

# 11  Slioch, Fisherfield, Dundonnell, and the Fannaichs

*Beinn a'Chlaidheimh, Sgurr Ban and Mullach Coire Mhic Fhearchair*

## Slioch                                                    3217ft/980m

The spear

Distance_____ Miles/Km   Height_____ ft/m   Date\_\_\_/\_\_\_/\_\_\_

Weather      _____

Companions   _____

Route        _____

and Notes    _____

_____

_____

_____

_____

_____

_____

## A'Mhaighdean                                              3173ft/967m

The maiden

Distance_____ Miles/Km   Height_____ ft/m   Date\_\_\_/\_\_\_/\_\_\_

Weather      _____

Companions   _____

Route        _____

and Notes    _____

_____

_____

_____

_____

_____

_____

| **Ruadh Stac Mor** | **3014ft/918m★** |

Big red peak

Distance_____ Miles/Km   Height_____ ft/m   Date___/___/___

Weather   _____

Companions _____

Route    _____

and Notes  _____

_____

_____

_____

_____

_____

_____

_____

| **Beinn Tarsuinn** | **3070ft/936m★★** |

The transverse or crosswise mountain

Distance_____ Miles/Km   Height_____ ft/m   Date___/___/___

Weather   _____

Companions _____

Route    _____

and Notes  _____

_____

_____

_____

_____

_____

_____

★ Recognised as over 3000ft from O.S. 1:50 000 map – entered to revised Munro's list 1974.
★★ Confirmed as over 3000ft from O.S. 1:50 000 map and entered to Munro's revised list 1974.

## Mullach Coire Mhic Fhearchair               3326ft/1019m

The top of the son of Farquhar's corrie

Distance_____ Miles/Km   Height_____ ft/m   Date____/____/____

Weather     _____

Companions  _____

Route        _____

and Notes    _____

_____

_____

_____

_____

_____

_____

_____

## Sgurr Ban                          3194ft/989m

The white peak

Distance_____ Miles/Km   Height_____ ft/m   Date____/____/____

Weather     _____

Companions  _____

Route        _____

and Notes    _____

_____

_____

_____

_____

_____

_____

_____

| **Beinn a'Chlaidheimh** | **3000ft/914m★** |
|---|---|

Mountain of the sword

Distance_____ Miles/Km   Height_____ ft/m   Date___/___/___

Weather _____

Companions _____

Route _____

and Notes _____

_____

_____

_____

_____

_____

_____

_____

_____

## The Fisherfield Peaks

For many years the number of Munros was said to be 276, with a note to suggest that Beinn Tarsuinn should be considered a serious contender for inclusion in the list. This was based on several observations by members of the S.M.C. who estimated a height of about 3080ft. Mr Colin Phillip noted, "The map of this part was very casual; I think the O.S. had bad weather, and were hurried in order to meet the views of the then laird".

The two hills of Ruadh Stac Mor and Beinn a' Chlaidheimh certainly fell into the category of casual survey as the 1″ maps up to 1968 showed only a contour of 2850ft for Ruadh Stac Mor and 2800ft for Beinn a'Chlaidheimh, the latter having the appearance of a very level summit, whereas it has a narrow undulating summit ridge. Even at this late juncture the upper contour of Beinn Tarsuinn was still set at 2850ft.

The second series O.S. 1:50 000 maps give firm heights for Beinn a'Chlaidheimh ★(914m, entered to revised Munro's list in 1974), and Ruadh Stac Mor (918m), the latter now being more firmly established as a triangulation point carrying an Ordnance Survey pillar, used on the metric map triangulations. Beinn Tarsuinn within a 930m contour, confirms the accuracy of earlier observations by the members of the S.M.C.

## An Teallach – Bidein a'Ghlas Thuill                    3484ft/1062m

The forge – the sharp peak of the hollow

Distance_____ Miles/Km  Height_____ ft/m  Date____/____/____

Weather      _____

Companions   _____

Route        _____

and Notes    _____

_____

_____

_____

_____

_____

_____

_____


## An Teallach – Sgurr Fiona                             3474ft/1059m*

The forge – Peak of the wine

Distance_____ Miles/Km  Height_____ ft/m  Date____/____/____

Weather      _____

Companions   _____

Route        _____

and Notes    _____

_____

_____

_____

_____

_____

_____

* Entered to revised Munro's list 1980.

| **A'Chailleach** | **3276ft/999m** |

The old woman

Distance_____ Miles/Km   Height_____ ft/m   Date___/___/____

Weather _____

Companions _____

Route _____

and Notes _____

_____

_____

_____

_____

_____

_____

_____


| **Sgurr Breac** | **3281ft/1000m** |

The speckled crag

Distance_____ Miles/Km   Height_____ ft/m   Date___/___/____

Weather _____

Companions _____

Route _____

and Notes _____

_____

_____

_____

_____

_____

_____

_____

## Meall a'Chrasgaidh                                    3062ft/934m

Hill of the crossing

Distance_____ Miles/Km   Height_____ ft/m   Date\_\_\_/\_\_\_/\_\_\_

Weather

Companions

Route

and Notes

## Sgurr Mor                                              3637ft/1110m

The great peak

Distance_____ Miles/Km   Height_____ ft/m   Date\_\_\_/\_\_\_/\_\_\_

Weather

Companions

Route

and Notes

## Sgurr nan Clach Geala                               3581ft/1093m

The peak of the white stones

Distance_____ Miles/Km   Height_____ ft/m   Date____/____/____

Weather   _____

Companions _____

Route   _____

and Notes   _____

_____

_____

_____

_____

_____

_____

_____

## Sgurr nan Each                                      3026ft/923m

The horses' peak

Distance_____ Miles/Km   Height_____ ft/m   Date____/____/____

Weather   _____

Companions _____

Route   _____

and Notes   _____

_____

_____

_____

_____

_____

_____

_____

## Meall Gorm
3174ft/949m

Green hill

Distance_____ Miles/Km   Height_____ ft/m   Date___/___/___

Weather        _____

Companions     _____

Route          _____

and Notes      _____

_____

_____

_____

_____

_____

_____

_____

_____

## An Coileachan
3015ft/923m

The cockerel

Distance_____ Miles/Km   Height_____ ft/m   Date___/___/___

Weather        _____

Companions     _____

Route          _____

and Notes      _____

_____

_____

_____

_____

_____

_____

_____

_____

129

## Beinn Liath Mhor Fannaich                                    3129ft/954m
### Big grey mountain of Fannich

Distance_____ Miles/Km   Height_____ ft/m   Date___/___/___

Weather _____

Companions _____

Route _____

and Notes _____

_____

_____

_____

_____

_____

_____

_____

_____


## Fionn Bheinn                                                 3062ft/933m
### The white mountain

Distance_____ Miles/Km   Height_____ ft/m   Date___/___/___

Weather _____

Companions _____

Route _____

and Notes _____

_____

_____

_____

_____

_____

_____

_____

# 12 Wyvis, Strathvaick, Inverlael

*Beinn Dearg and Cona'Mheall*

## Ben Wyvis – Glas Leathad Mor                         3433ft/1046m

The noble or awesome mountain – The big, green, grassy slope

Distance_____ Miles/Km   Height_____ ft/m   Date___/___/___

Weather    _____

Companions _____

Route      _____

and Notes  _____

_____

_____

_____

_____

_____

_____

_____

_____


## Am Faochagach                                        3120ft/954m

The whelk shaped mountain

Distance_____ Miles/Km   Height_____ ft/m   Date___/___/___

Weather    _____

Companions _____

Route      _____

and Notes  _____

_____

_____

_____

_____

_____

_____

_____

## Cona'Mheall                                          3214ft/980m

The enchanted hill

Distance_____ Miles/Km   Height_____ ft/m   Date___/___/___

Weather       _____

Companions    _____

Route         _____

and Notes     _____

_____

_____

_____

_____

_____

_____

_____


## Beinn Dearg                                          3547ft/1084m

The red mountain

Distance_____ Miles/Km   Height_____ ft/m   Date___/___/___

Weather       _____

Companions    _____

Route         _____

and Notes     _____

_____

_____

_____

_____

_____

_____

_____

## Meall nan Ceapraichean          3205ft/977m

The hill of the stumps or little tops

Distance_____ Miles/Km   Height_____ ft/m   Date____/____/____

Weather _____

Companions _____

Route _____

and Notes _____

_____

_____

_____

_____

_____

_____

_____

_____

## Eididh nan Clach Geala          3039ft/928m

The covering of white stones

Distance_____ Miles/Km   Height_____ ft/m   Date____/____/____

Weather _____

Companions _____

Route _____

and Notes _____

_____

_____

_____

_____

_____

_____

_____

_____

134

**Seana Bhraigh**                                         **3040ft/927m**

Old mountain or hill

Distance_____ Miles/Km   Height_____ ft/m   Date____/____/____

Weather _____

Companions _____

Route _____

and Notes _____

_____

_____

_____

_____

_____

_____

_____

_____

_____

# 13  Assynt and the far north

Ben Hope

## Ben More Assynt                                3273ft/998m

The great mountain of Assynt

Distance_____ Miles/Km    Height_____ ft/m    Date____/____/____

Weather

Companions

Route

and Notes

## Conival                                       3234ft/987m

The enchanted hill

Distance_____ Miles/Km    Height_____ ft/m    Date____/____/____

Weather

Companions

Route

and Notes

137

## Ben Klibreck – Meall nan Con 3154ft/961m

The mountain of the speckled stones – The hill of the dogs

Distance_____ Miles/Km  Height_____ ft/m  Date____/____/____

Weather  _____

Companions  _____

Route  _____

and Notes  _____

_____

_____

_____

_____

_____

_____

_____

## Ben Hope 3042ft/927m

The mountain of the bay

Distance_____ Miles/Km  Height_____ ft/m  Date____/____/____

Weather  _____

Companions  _____

Route  _____

and Notes  _____

_____

_____

_____

_____

_____

_____

_____

138

# 14   The Cairngorms

*Carn a'Mhaim and Ben Macdui*

## Ben Avon – Leabaidh an Daimh Bhuidhe                    3843ft/1171m
Mountain of the ford of Fionn – The couch of the yellow stag

Distance_____ Miles/Km   Height_____ ft/m   Date____/____/____

Weather         _____

Companions      _____

Route           _____

and Notes       _____

_____

_____

_____

_____

_____

_____

_____

_____


## Beinn a'Bhuird                                          3924ft/1196m
Table hill

Distance_____ Miles/Km   Height_____ ft/m   Date____/____/____

Weather         _____

Companions      _____

Route           _____

and Notes       _____

_____

_____

_____

_____

_____

_____

_____

_____

## Beinn Bhreac                                        3051ft/931m
#### Speckled mountain

Distance_____ Miles/Km   Height_____ ft/m   Date____/____/____

Weather     _____

Companions  _____

Route       _____

and Notes   _____

_____

_____

_____

_____

_____

_____

_____

_____


## Beinn a'Chaorainn                                   3553ft/1082m
#### Mountain of the rowan tree

Distance_____ Miles/Km   Height_____ ft/m   Date____/____/____

Weather     _____

Companions  _____

Route       _____

and Notes   _____

_____

_____

_____

_____

_____

_____

_____

_____

## Bynack More                           3574ft/1090m

Big band, kerchief or cap

Distance_____ Miles/Km   Height_____ ft/m   Date___/___/___

Weather   _____

Companions  _____

Route      _____

and Notes   _____

_____

_____

_____

_____

_____

_____

_____

_____

## A'Choinneach                        3345ft/1017m★

The moss

Distance_____ Miles/Km   Height_____ ft/m   Date___/___/___

Weather   _____

Companions  _____

Route      _____

and Notes   _____

_____

_____

_____

_____

_____

_____

★ Deleted from Munro's list in 1980.

142

## Beinn Mheadhoin 3883ft/1182m

Middle mountain

Distance_____ Miles/Km   Height_____ ft/m   Date____/____/____

Weather _____

Companions _____

Route _____

and Notes _____

_____

_____

_____

_____

_____

_____

_____

## Derry Cairngorm 3788ft/1155m

The blue cairn of Derry

Distance_____ Miles/Km   Height_____ ft/m   Date____/____/____

Weather _____

Companions _____

Route _____

and Notes _____

_____

_____

_____

_____

_____

_____

_____

143

## Carn a'Mhaim — 3402ft/1064m

Cairn of the large rounded hill

Distance_____ Miles/Km   Height_____ ft/m   Date____/____/____

Weather _____

Companions _____

Route _____

and Notes _____

_____

_____

_____

_____

_____

_____

_____

_____

## Ben Macdui — 4296ft/1309m

Macduff's hill

Distance_____ Miles/Km   Height_____ ft/m   Date____/____/____

Weather _____

Companions _____

Route _____

and Notes _____

_____

_____

_____

_____

_____

_____

_____

_____

## Cairn Gorm                                             4084ft/1245m

The blue cairn

Distance_____ Miles/Km    Height_____ ft/m    Date____/____/____

Weather         _____

Companions      _____

Route           _____

and Notes       _____

_____

_____

_____

_____

_____

_____

_____


## Braeriach (Braigh Riabhach)                            4248ft/1296m

Brindled or speckled upland

Distance_____ Miles/Km    Height_____ ft/m    Date____/____/____

Weather         _____

Companions      _____

Route           _____

and Notes       _____

_____

_____

_____

_____

_____

_____

_____

## Cairn Toul        4241ft/1291m

Hill of the barn

Distance_____ Miles/Km   Height_____ ft/m   Date\_\_\_/\_\_\_/\_\_\_

Weather _____

Companions _____

Route _____

and Notes _____

## The Devil's Point        3303ft/1004m

Translation from Bod an Deamhain

Distance_____ Miles/Km   Height_____ ft/m   Date\_\_\_/\_\_\_/\_\_\_

Weather _____

Companions _____

Route _____

and Notes _____

| **Beinn Bhrotain** | 3795ft/1157m |

Hill of Brodan

Distance_____ Miles/Km   Height_____ ft/m   Date____/____/____

Weather     _____

Companions  _____

Route       _____

and Notes   _____

_____

_____

_____

_____

_____

_____

_____

_____


| **Monadh Mor** | 3651ft/1113m |

Big hill

Distance_____ Miles/Km   Height_____ ft/m   Date____/____/____

Weather     _____

Companions  _____

Route       _____

and Notes   _____

_____

_____

_____

_____

_____

_____

_____

_____

| Carn Cloich-mhuilinn | 3087ft/942m* |

Hill of the millstone

Distance_____ Miles/Km   Height_____ ft/m   Date\_\_\_/\_\_\_/\_\_\_

Weather _____

Companions _____

Route _____

and Notes _____

* Deleted from Munro's list in 1980.

### "The last Munro"

It is somewhat ironical that of all the mountains which have become so associated with the lists of Sir Hugh T. Munro, Carn Cloich-mhuilinn should have suffered demotion to a "top" in the revisions of 1980. This was to have been Munro's last mountain ascent on his round of the 3000ft peaks. Before his untimely death he had decided to invite his many friends in the S.M.C. to accompany him, and had arranged that a suitable celebratory luncheon be taken up to the cairn by pony.

Even had the 1980 revisions been based on a definite 250ft ascent on all sides, the mountain would have still failed to qualify by the narrow margin of 4ft. Observations from the O.S. 1:25 000 Outdoor Leisure map of the Cairngorms shows a spot height of 867m at the centre of the col separating the hill from its higher neighbour, Beinn Bhrotain. The reascent to the cairn at 942m is therefore 75m (246ft).

## Mullach Clach a'Bhlair                    3338ft/1019m
### Summit stone of the plain

Distance_____ Miles/Km   Height_____ ft/m   Date____/____/____

Weather       _____

Companions  _____

Route         _____

and Notes    _____

_____

_____

_____

_____

_____

_____

_____


## Meall Dubhag                              3268ft/998m*
### Lump of the black field

Distance_____ Miles/Km   Height_____ ft/m   Date____/____/____

Weather       _____

Companions  _____

Route         _____

and Notes    _____

_____

_____

_____

_____

_____

_____

* Deleted from Munro's list in 1980.

## Carn Ban Mor                      3443ft/1052m★

Big, fair hill

Distance_____ Miles/Km    Height_____ ft/m   Date___/___/___

Weather _____

Companions _____

Route _____

and Notes _____

_____

_____

_____

_____

_____

_____

_____

## Sgor Gaoith                       3658ft/1118m

Peak of the wind

Distance_____ Miles/Km    Height_____ ft/m   Date___/___/___

Weather _____

Companions _____

Route _____

and Notes _____

_____

_____

_____

_____

_____

_____

★ Deleted from Munro's list in 1980.

| **Geal Charn** | | | 3019ft/920m★ |
|---|---|---|---|

White hill

Distance_____ Miles/Km    Height_____ ft/m    Date____/____/____

Weather         _____

Companions     _____

Route           _____

and Notes       _____

_____

_____

_____

_____

_____

_____

_____

_____

★ Deleted from Munro's list in 1980.

# 15  Gaick, Atholl, Glen Ey
# and the Cairnwell

*Carn a'Chlamain and Glen Tilt*

## Meall Chuaich             3120ft/951m

Cup lump

Distance_____ Miles/Km   Height_____ ft/m   Date____/____/____

Weather

Companions

Route

and Notes

## Carn na Caim             3087ft/941m

Hill of the twist

Distance_____ Miles/Km   Height_____ ft/m   Date____/____/____

Weather

Companions

Route

and Notes

## A'Bhuidheanach Bheag                                    3064ft/936m
The little yellow place

Distance_____ Miles/Km   Height_____ ft/m   Date____/____/____

Weather      _____

Companions   _____

Route        _____

and Notes    _____

_____

_____

_____

_____

_____

_____

_____

_____


## Beinn Dearg                                            3304ft/1008m
Red hill

Distance_____ Miles/Km   Height_____ ft/m   Date____/____/____

Weather      _____

Companions   _____

Route        _____

and Notes    _____

_____

_____

_____

_____

_____

_____

_____

## Carn an Fhidhleir (Carn Ealar)                    3276ft/994m
Hill of the fiddler

Distance_____ Miles/Km   Height_____ ft/m   Date____/____/____

Weather     _____

Companions  _____

Route       _____

and Notes   _____

_____

_____

_____

_____

_____

_____

_____

_____


## An Sgarsoch                                        3300ft/1006m
The place of sharp rocks

Distance_____ Miles/Km   Height_____ ft/m   Date____/____/____

Weather     _____

Companions  _____

Route       _____

and Notes   _____

_____

_____

_____

_____

_____

_____

_____

155

## Carn a'Chlamain                                    3159ft/963m

Hill of the kite or buzzard

Distance_____ Miles/Km   Height_____ ft/m   Date___/___/___

Weather _____

Companions _____

Route _____

and Notes _____

_____

_____

_____

_____

_____

_____

_____


## Beinn a'Ghlo – Carn nan Gabhar                      3677ft/1129m

Mountain of the mist or veil – Hill of the goats

Distance_____ Miles/Km   Height_____ ft/m   Date___/___/___

Weather _____

Companions _____

Route _____

and Notes _____

_____

_____

_____

_____

_____

_____

_____

## Beinn a'Ghlo – Braigh Coire Chruinn-bhalgain          3505ft/1070m

Mountain of the mist or veil – Upland of the corrie of the round, little blisters

Distance_____ Miles/Km   Height_____ ft/m   Date____/____/____

Weather      _____

Companions   _____

Route        _____

and Notes    _____

_____

_____

_____

_____

_____

_____

_____


## Beinn a'Ghlo – Carn Liath          3197ft/975m

Mountain of the mist or veil – Grey hill

Distance_____ Miles/Km   Height_____ ft/m   Date____/____/____

Weather      _____

Companions   _____

Route        _____

and Notes    _____

_____

_____

_____

_____

_____

_____

_____

157

| Carn an Righ | 3377ft/1029m |
|---|---|

Hill of the king (Malcolm II 1058-93)

Distance_____ Miles/Km   Height_____ ft/m   Date____/____/____

Weather      _____

Companions _____

Route        _____

and Notes    _____

_____

_____

_____

_____

_____

_____

_____

_____

| Glas Tulaichean | 3449ft/1051m |
|---|---|

Green hill

Distance_____ Miles/Km   Height_____ ft/m   Date____/____/____

Weather      _____

Companions _____

Route        _____

and Notes    _____

_____

_____

_____

_____

_____

_____

_____

158

## Beinn Iutharn Mhor           3424ft/1045m

Big Hell's peak

Distance_____ Miles/Km   Height_____ ft/m   Date___/___/___

Weather     _____

Companions   _____

Route        _____

and Notes    _____

_____

_____

_____

_____

_____

_____

_____


## Carn Bhac           3098ft/946m

Hill of the peat banks

Distance_____ Miles/Km   Height_____ ft/m   Date___/___/___

Weather     _____

Companions   _____

Route        _____

and Notes    _____

_____

_____

_____

_____

_____

_____

_____

159

## An Socach 3073ft/944m

The snout

Distance_____ Miles/Km   Height_____ ft/m   Date____/____/____

Weather     _____

Companions  _____

Route       _____

and Notes   _____

_____

_____

_____

_____

_____

_____

_____

## Carn a'Gheoidh 3194ft/975m

Hill of the goose

Distance_____ Miles/Km   Height_____ ft/m   Date____/____/____

Weather     _____

Companions  _____

Route       _____

and Notes   _____

_____

_____

_____

_____

_____

_____

_____

## The Cairnwell (An Carn Bhalg)                  3059ft/933m
Hill of blisters

Distance_____ Miles/Km   Height_____ ft/m   Date____/____/____

Weather      _____

Companions  _____

Route        _____

and Notes    _____

_____

_____

_____

_____

_____

_____

_____


## Carn Aosda                                    3003ft/917m
Hill of age

Distance_____ Miles/Km   Height_____ ft/m   Date____/____/____

Weather      _____

Companions  _____

Route        _____

and Notes    _____

_____

_____

_____

_____

_____

_____

_____

# 16   Lochnagar and east of the Devil's Elbow

*Broad Cairn and Creag an Dubh Loch*

## Glas Maol                                          3504ft/1068m

The green lump

Distance_____ Miles/Km   Height_____ ft/m   Date____/____/____

Weather      _____

Companions   _____

Route        _____

and Notes    _____

_____

_____

_____

_____

_____

_____

_____


## Creag Leacach                                      3238ft/987m

Slabby rock

Distance_____ Miles/Km   Height_____ ft/m   Date____/____/____

Weather      _____

Companions   _____

Route        _____

and Notes    _____

_____

_____

_____

_____

_____

_____

_____

## Cairn of Claise (Carn na Glasha)      3484ft/1064m

Hill of the hollow

Distance_____ Miles/Km   Height_____ ft/m   Date____/____/____

Weather   _____

Companions   _____

Route   _____

and Notes   _____

_____

_____

_____

_____

_____

_____

_____


## Carn an Tuirc      3340ft/1019m

Hill of the boar

Distance_____ Miles/Km   Height_____ ft/m   Date____/____/____

Weather   _____

Companions   _____

Route   _____

and Notes   _____

_____

_____

_____

_____

_____

_____

_____

164

| **Tom Buidhe** | **3140ft/957m** |
|---|---|

Yellow knoll

Distance_____ Miles/Km   Height_____ ft/m   Date____/____/____

Weather _____

Companions _____

Route _____

and Notes _____

_____

_____

_____

_____

_____

_____

_____

| **Tolmount** | **3143ft/958m** |
|---|---|

Valley hill

Distance_____ Miles/Km   Height_____ ft/m   Date____/____/____

Weather _____

Companions _____

Route _____

and Notes _____

_____

_____

_____

_____

_____

_____

_____

## Cairn Bannoch (Carn Beannach)     3314ft/1012m

Peaked hill

Distance_____ Miles/Km   Height_____ ft/m   Date___/___/___

Weather _____

Companions _____

Route _____

and Notes _____

_____

_____

_____

_____

_____

_____

_____


## Broad Cairn (Cairn Braghaid)     3268ft/998m

Hill of upland

Distance_____ Miles/Km   Height_____ ft/m   Date___/___/___

Weather _____

Companions _____

Route _____

and Notes _____

_____

_____

_____

_____

_____

_____

_____

## Lochnagar (Beinn Cichean)      3789ft/1155m

Tarn of the noise, sobbing or goats (Mountain of the teats)

Distance_____ Miles/Km   Height_____ ft/m   Date\_\_\_/\_\_\_/\_\_\_

Weather _____

Companions _____

Route _____

and Notes _____

---
---
---
---
---
---
---

## The White Mounth – Carn a'Choire Bhoidheach      3650ft/1110m

Cairn of the beautiful corrie

Distance_____ Miles/Km   Height_____ ft/m   Date\_\_\_/\_\_\_/\_\_\_

Weather _____

Companions _____

Route _____

and Notes _____

---
---
---
---
---
---
---
---

## Carn an t-Sagairt Mor                              3430ft/1047m
Big hill of the priest

Distance_____ Miles/Km   Height_____ ft/m   Date____/____/____

Weather         _____

Companions      _____

Route           _____

and Notes       _____

_____

_____

_____

_____

_____

_____

_____


## Mount Keen (Monadh Caoin)                          3077ft/939m
Pleasant hill

Distance_____ Miles/Km   Height_____ ft/m   Date____/____/____

Weather         _____

Companions      _____

Route           _____

and Notes       _____

_____

_____

_____

_____

_____

_____

_____

## Driesh                                                    3108ft/947m

Bramble place

Distance_____ Miles/Km   Height_____ ft/m   Date____/____/____

Weather

Companions

Route

and Notes


## Mayar                                                     3043ft/928m

My delight or the plain

Distance_____ Miles/Km   Height_____ ft/m   Date____/____/____

Weather

Companions

Route

and Notes

# 17   Skye and Mull

*Sgurr Dearg, Sgurr na Banachdich and Sgurr a'Ghreadaidh*

## Bla Bheinn (Blaven)                     3044ft/928m

The hill of bloom

Distance_____ Miles/Km   Height_____ ft/m   Date___/___/___

Weather      _____

Companions   _____

Route        _____

and Notes    _____

_____

_____

_____

_____

_____

_____

_____

_____


## Sgurr nan Gillean                       3167ft/965m

The peak of the young men

Distance_____ Miles/Km   Height_____ ft/m   Date___/___/___

Weather      _____

Companions   _____

Route        _____

and Notes    _____

_____

_____

_____

_____

_____

_____

_____

## Am Basteir
**3069ft/935m**

The executioner

Distance_____ Miles/Km   Height_____ ft/m   Date____/____/____

Weather    _____

Companions  _____

Route      _____

and Notes   _____

_____

_____

_____

_____

_____

_____

_____

_____


## Bruach na Frithe
**3143ft/958m**

The brae of the forest

Distance_____ Miles/Km   Height_____ ft/m   Date____/____/____

Weather    _____

Companions  _____

Route      _____

and Notes   _____

_____

_____

_____

_____

_____

_____

_____

_____

## Sgurr a'Mhadaidh                                              3010ft/918m

The fox's peak

Distance_____ Miles/Km   Height_____ ft/m   Date____/____/____

Weather        _____

Companions     _____

Route          _____

and Notes      _____

_____

_____

_____

_____

_____

_____

_____

_____


## Sgurr a'Ghreadaidh                                            3197ft/973m

Peak of the thrashing or mighty winds

Distance_____ Miles/Km   Height_____ ft/m   Date____/____/____

Weather        _____

Companions     _____

Route          _____

and Notes      _____

_____

_____

_____

_____

_____

_____

_____

## Sgurr na Banachdich                          3167ft/965m

Smallpox peak, or peak of the milkmaid

Distance_____ Miles/Km   Height_____ ft/m   Date___/___/___

Weather

Companions

Route

and Notes

## Sgurr Dearg – Inaccessible Pinnacle          3254ft/986m

Red peak

Distance_____ Miles/Km   Height_____ ft/m   Date___/___/___

Weather

Companions

Route

and Notes

## Sgurr Mhic Choinnich                                    3107ft/948m

MacKenzie's peak

Distance_____ Miles/Km   Height_____ ft/m   Date\_\_\_/\_\_\_/\_\_\_

Weather

Companions

Route

and Notes

## Sgurr Alasdair                                          3309ft/993m

Peak of Alexander (Nicolson)

Distance_____ Miles/Km   Height_____ ft/m   Date\_\_\_/\_\_\_/\_\_\_

Weather

Companions

Route

and Notes

## Sgurr Dubh Mor                                      3089ft/944m
Big black peak

Distance_____ Miles/Km  Height_____ ft/m  Date___/___/___

Weather _____

Companions _____

Route _____

and Notes _____

_____

_____

_____

_____

_____

_____

_____

_____


## Sgurr nan Eag                                       3037ft/924m
The notched peak

Distance_____ Miles/Km  Height_____ ft/m  Date___/___/___

Weather _____

Companions _____

Route _____

and Notes _____

_____

_____

_____

_____

_____

_____

_____

## Ben More (Mull)               3169ft/966m

The big mountain

Distance_____ Miles/Km   Height_____ ft/m   Date\_\_\_\_/\_\_\_\_/\_\_\_\_

Weather

Companions

Route

and Notes

# Appendix A

## Section 1

Ben Lomond    3192ft/974m
Beinn Narnain    3036ft/926m
Beinn Ime    3318ft/1011m
Ben Vane    3004ft/916m
Ben Vorlich    3092ft/943m
Beinn Buidhe    3106ft/948m
Beinn a'Chleibh    3008ft/917m
Beinn Laoigh (Ben Lui)    3708ft/1130m
Ben Oss    3374ft/1028m
Beinn Dubhchraig    3204ft/977m
Beinn Chabhair    3053ft/931m
An Caisteal    3265ft/995m
Beinn a'Chroin    3104ft/940m
Beinn Tulaichean    3099ft/945m
Cruach Ardrain    3248ft/1045m
Stob Garbh    3148ft/960m*
Ben More    3843ft/1174m
Stob Binnein (Stobinian)    3821ft/1165m
Meall na Dige    3140ft/966m*

Total 19

## Section 2

Ben Vorlich    3231ft/985m
Stuc a'Chroin    3189ft/972m
Ben Chonzie    3048ft/931m

Total 3

**Section 3**

Schiehallion   3547ft/1083m
Carn Mairg   3419ft/1042m
Creag Mhor   3200ft/981m
Carn Gorm   3370ft/1029m
Meall Garbh   3200ft/963m
Ben Lawers   3984ft/1214m
An Stuc +   3643ft/1118m*
Beinn Ghlas   3657ft/1103m
Meall Greigh   3280ft/1001m
Meall Garbh   3661ft/1118m
Meall Corranaich 3530ft/1069m
Meall a'Choire Leith   3033ft/926m
Meall nan Tarmachan   3421ft/1043m
Beinn nan Eachan   3265ft/995m*
Meall Ghaordaidh   3410ft/1039m
Stuchd an Lochain   3144ft/960m
Meall Buidhe   3054ft/931m
Beinn Heasgarnich   3530ft/1076m
Creag Mhor   3387ft/1032m
Ben Challum   3354ft/1022m
Meall Glas   3139ft/957m
Beinn Cheathaich   3076ft/937m*
Sgiath Chuil   3016ft/919m
Beinn Dorain   3524ft/1074m
Beinn an Dothaidh   3289ft/1002m
Beinn Achaladair   3404ft/1038m
Beinn a'Chreachain   3540ft/1081m
Beinn Mhanach   3125ft/953m

Total 28

+ Reclassified as mountain in the *Munro's Tables* of 1997.

# Section 4

Ben Cruachan   3695ft/1126m
Stob Dearg (Taynuilt Peak)   3611ft/1101m*
Meall Cuanail   3004ft/916m*
Stob Diamh   3272ft/997m
Beinn a'Chochuill   3215ft/980m
Beinn Eunaich   3242ft/988m
Ben Starav   3541ft/1078m
Glas Bheinn Mhor   3258ft/993m
Beinn nan Aighenan   3141ft/957m
Stob Coir'an Albannaich   3425ft/1044m
Meall nan Eun   3039ft/926m
Stob Ghabhar   3565ft/1087m
Stob a'Choire Odhair   3058ft/947m
Creise   3608ft/1100m
Meall a'Bhuiridh   3636ft/1108m
Buachaille Etive Mor - Stob Dearg   3345ft/1022m
Buachaille Etive Mor - Stob na Doire   3316ft/1011m*
Buachaille Etive Mor - Stob na Broige +   3120ft/955m*
Buachaille Etive Beag - Stob Dubh   3129ft/958m
Buachaille Etive Beag - Stob Coire Raineach +   3029ft/924m*
Bidean nam Bian - Main Summit   3766ft/1150m
Bidean nam Bian - Stob Coire nan Lochan   3657ft/1115m*
Bidean nam Bian - Stob Coire Sgreamhach +   3497ft/1070m*
Sgor na h-Ulaidh   3258ft/994m
Stob an Fhuarain   3160ft/910m*
Beinn Fhionnlaidh   3145ft/959m
Beinn Sgulaird   3059ft/932m
Beinn a'Bheithir – Sgorr Dhearg 3361ft/1024m
Beinn a'Bheithir – Sgorr Dhonuill   3284ft/1001m

Total 29

+ Reclassified as mountain in the *Munro's Tables* of 1997.

## Section 5

Aonach Eagach – Sgorr nam Fiannaidh   3173ft/967m
Aonach Eagach – Meall Dearg   3118ft/951m
Sgurr Eilde Mor   3279ft/1008m
Binnein Beag   3083ft/940m
Binnein Mor   3700ft/1128m
Na Gruagaichean   3442ft/1055m
An Gearanach   3230ft/985m
Stob Coire a'Chairn   3219ft/983m
Am Bodach   3382ft/1034m
Sgurr a'Mhaim   3601ft/1098m
Sgor an Iubhair ‡   3284ft/1001m
Stob Ban   3274ft/999m
Mullach nan Coirean   3077ft/939m
Ben Nevis   4406ft/1344m
Carn Mor Dearg   4012ft/1223m
Aonach Mor   3999ft/1219m
Aonach Beag   4060ft/1236m
Sgurr Choinnich Mor   3603ft/1095m
Stob Choire Claurigh   3858ft/1177m
Stob Ban   3217ft/977m
Stob Coire Easain   3658ft/1116m
Stob a'Choire Mheadhoin   3610ft/1106m
Stob Coire Sgriodain   3211ft/976m
Chno Dearg   3433ft/1047m
Beinn na Lap   3066ft/937m
Carn Dearg   3080ft/941m
Sgor Gaibhre   3124ft/955m
Sgor Choinnich   3040ft/929m*
Beinn Eibhinn   3611ft/1100m
Aonach Beag   3647ft/1114m
Geal Charn   3656ft/1132m
Carn Dearg   3391ft/1034m
Beinn a'Chlachair   3569ft/1088m
Mullach Coire an Iubhair (Geal Charn)   3443ft/1049m
Creag Pitridh   3031ft/924m
Ben Alder   3765ft/1148m
Beinn Bheoil   3333ft/1019m
Sgairneach Mor   3251ft/991m
Beinn Udlamain   3306ft/1010m
A'Mharconaich   3185ft/975m
Geal-charn   3005ft/917m

Total 41

‡ Demoted to Top in the *Munro's Tables* of 1997.

## Section 6

Beinn Teallach    2994ft/915m
Beinn a'Chaorainn    3453ft/1052m
Creag Meagaidh    3700ft/1130m
Stob Poite Coire Ardair    3460ft/1053m
Carn Liath    3298ft/1006m
Carn Dearg    3093ft/945m
A'Chailleach    3054ft/930m
Geal Charn    3036ft/926m

Total 8


## Section 7

Sron a'Choire Ghairbh    3066ft/935m
Meall na Teanga    3010ft/917m
Gaor Bheinn (Gulvain)    3224ft/987m
Gaor Bheinn (Gulvain) (South top)    3155ft/962m*
Sgurr Thuilm    3164ft/963m
Sgurr nan Coireachan    3136ft/956m
Sgurr na Ciche    3410ft/1040m
Garbh Chioch Mhor    3365ft/1013m
Sgurr nan Coireachan    3125ft/953m
Sgurr Mor    3290ft/1003m
Gairich    3015ft/919m
Meall Buidhe    3107ft/946m
Luinne Bheinn    3083ft/939m
Ladhar Bheinn    3343ft/1020m
Beinn Sgritheall (Ben Sgriol)    3196ft/974m
The Saddle    3317ft/1010m
Sgurr na Sgine    3098ft/945m
Sgurr a'Mhaoraich    3365ft/1027m
Gleouraich    3395ft/1035m
Spidean Mialach    3268ft/996m
Creag a'Mhaim    3102ft/947m
Druim Shionnach    3222ft/987m
Aonach air Chrith    3342ft/1021m
Maol Chinn-dearg    3214ft/981m
Sgurr an Doire Leathain    3272ft/1010m
Sgurr an Lochain    3282ft/1004m
Creag nan Damh    3012ft/918m

Total 27

## Section 8

Sgurr nan Saighead   3050ft/929m*
Sgurr Fhuaran   3505ft/1068m
Sgurr na Carnach +   3270ft/1002m*
Sgurr na Ciste Duibhe   3370ft/1027m
Saileag   3124ft/959m
Sgurr a'Bhealaich Dheirg   3378ft/1031m
Aonach Meadhoin   3284ft/1003m
Ciste Dhubh   3218ft/982m
Mullach Fraoch-choire   3614ft/1102m
A'Chralaig   3673ft/1120m
Tigh Mor na Seilge (Sail Chaorainn)   3285ft/1002m
Sgurr nan Conbhairean   3635ft/1109m
A'Ghlas-bheinn   3006ft/918m
Beinn Fhada (Ben Attow)   3385ft/1032m
Sgurr nan Ceathreamhnan   3771ft/1151m
Creag a'Choir'Aird
Mullach na Dheiragain (also Creag a'Choir'Aird (South top))   3210ft/982m
Mullach na Dheiragain (South top) – formerly un-named summit of Creag
a'Choir'Aird (also known as Carn na Con Dhu) (073242)   3176ft/968m*
An Socach   3017ft/920m
Mam Sodhail (Mam Soul)   3862ft/1181m
Sgurr na Lapaich   3401ft/1036m*
Carn Eige (Eighe)   3880ft/1183m
Beinn Fhionnlaidh   3294ft/1005m
Tom a'Choinich   3646ft/1111m
Toll Creagach   3455ft/1053m

Total 24

+ Reclassified as mountain in the *Munro's Tables* of 1997.

## Section 9

Creag Dubh   3102ft/946m★
Carn nan Gobhar   3251ft/992m
Sgurr na Lapaich   3775ft/1150m
An Riabhachan   3696ft/1129m
An Socach   3508ft/1069m
Sgurr na Ruaidhe   3254ft/993m
Carn nan Gobhar   3255ft/992m
Sgurr a'Choire Ghlais   3554ft/1083m
Creag Ghorm a'Bhealaich   3378ft/1030m★
Sgurr Fhuar-thuill   3439ft/1049m
Maoile Lunndaidh   3304ft/1007m
Sgurr a'Chaorachain   3455ft/1053m
Bidean an Eoin Deirg   3430ft/1046m★
Sgurr Choinnich   3276ft/999m
Bidein a'Choire Sheasgaich   3102ft/945m
Lurg Mhor   3234ft/986m
Moruisg   3026ft/928m
Sgurr nan Ceannaichean   2896ft/915m

Total 18


## Section 10

Beinn Liath Mhor   3034ft/925m
Sgorr Ruadh   3142ft/960m
Maol Chean-dearg   3060ft/933m
Beinn Alligin – Sgurr Mhor   3232ft/985m
Beinn Alligin – Tom na Gruagaich +   3024ft/922m★
Liathach – Spidean a'Choire Leith   3456ft/1054m
Liathach – Mullach an Rathain   3358ft/1023m
Liathach – Stuc a'Choire Dhuibh Bhig   2995ft/915m★
Beinn Eighe – Ruadh-stac Mor   3309ft/1010m
Beinn Eighe – Sail Mhor   3217ft/981m★
Beinn Eighe – A'Choinneach Mhor   3130ft/954m★
Beinn Eighe - Spidean Coire nan Clach +   3188ft/972m★
Beinn Eighe – Sgurr nan Fhir Duibhe   3160ft/963m★

Total 13

184

+ Reclassified as mountain in the *Munro's Tables* of 1997.

## Section 11

Slioch 3217ft/980m
A'Mhaighdean 3173ft/967m
Ruadh Stac Mor 3014ft/918m
Beinn Tarsuinn 3070ft/936m
Mullach Coire Mhic Fhearchair 3326ft/1019m
Sgurr Ban 3194ft/989m
Beinn a'Chlaidheimh 3000ft/914m
An Teallach – Bidein a'Ghlas Thuill 3484ft/1062m
An Teallach – Sgurr Fiona 3474ft/1059m
An Teallach – Stob Cadha Gobhlach 3148ft/959m*
An Teallach – Glas Mheall Mhor 3217ft/981m*
An Teallach – Sgurr Creag an Eich 3335ft/1017m*
A'Chailleach 3276ft/999m
Sgurr Breac 3281ft/1000m
Meall a'Chrasgaidh 3062ft/934m
Sgurr Mor 3637ft/1110m
Sgurr na Clach Geala 3581ft/1093m
Sgurr nan Each 3026ft/923m
Meall Gorm 3174ft/949m
An Coileachan 3015ft/923m
Beinn Liath Mhor Fannaich 3129ft/954m
Fionn Bheinn 3062ft/933m

Total 22


## Section 12

Ben Wyvis – Glas Leathad Mor 3433ft/1046m
Ben Wyvis – Tom a'Choinnich 3134ft/955m*
Ben Wyvis – Glas Leathad Beag 3044ft/928m*
Am Faochagach 3120ft/954m
Cona'Mheall 3214ft/980m
Beinn Dearg 3547ft/1084m
Meall nan Ceapraichean 3205ft/977m
Eididh nan Clach Geala 3039ft/928m
Seana Bhraigh 3040ft/927m

Total 9

## Section 13

Ben More Assynt   3273ft/998m
Conival   3234ft/987m
Ben Klibreck – Meall nan Con   3154ft/961m
Ben Hope   3042ft/927m

Total 4


## Section 14

Ben Avon – Leabaidh an Daimh Bhuidhe   3843ft/1171m
Beinn a'Bhuird (North top)   3924ft/1196m
Beinn Bhreac   3051ft/931m
Beinn a'Chaorainn   3553ft/1082m
Bynack More   3574ft/1090m
A'Choinneach   3345ft/1017m*
Beinn Mheadhoin   3883ft/1182m
Derry Cairngorm   3788ft/1155m
Carn a'Mhaim   3402ft/1064m
Ben Macdui   4296ft/1309m
Cairn Gorm   4084ft/1245m
Cairn Lochan   3983ft/1215m*
Braeriach (Braigh Riabhach)   4248ft/1296m
Cairn Toul   4241ft/1291m
Sgor an Lochain Uaine (Angel's Peak) +   4150ft/1258m*
The Devil's Point   3303ft/1004m
Beinn Bhrotain   3795ft/1157m
Monadh Mor   3651ft/1113m
Mullach Clach a' Bhlair   3338ft/1019m
Sgor Gaoith   3658ft/1118m

Total 20

+ Reclassified as mountain in the *Munro's Tables* of 1997.

**Section 15**

Meall Chuaich   3120ft/951m
Carn na Caim   3087ft/941m
A'Bhuidheanach Bheag   3064ft/936m
Beinn Dearg   3304ft/1008m
Carn an Fhidhleir (Carn Ealar)   3276ft/994m
An Sgarsoch   3300ft/1006m
Carn a'Chlamain   3159ft/963m
Beinn a'Ghlo – Carn nan Gabhar   3677ft/1129m
Beinn a'Ghlo – Braigh Coire Chruinn-bhalgain   3505ft/1070m
Beinn a'Ghlo – Carn Liath   3197ft/975m
Carn an Righ   3377ft/1029m
Glas Tulaichean   3449ft/1051m
Beinn Iutharn Mhor   3424ft/1045m
Mam nan Carn   3224ft/986m*
Beinn Iutharn Bheag   3121ft/953m*
Carn Bhac   3098ft/946m
An Socach   3073ft/944m
Carn a'Gheoidh   3194ft/975m
The Cairnwell (An Carn Bhalg)   3059ft/933m
Carn Aosda   3003ft/917m

Total 20


**Section 16**

Glas Maol   3504ft/1068m
Cairn of Claise   3484ft/1064m
Cairn Bannoch (Carn Beannach)   3314ft/1012m
Lochnagar (Beinn Cichean) – Cac Carn Beag   3789ft/1155m
White Mounth – Carn a' Coire Boideach   3650ft/1110m
Carn an t-Sagairt Mor   3430ft/1047m
Mount Keen (Monadh Caoin)   3077ft/939m
Driesh   3108ft/947m
Mayar   3043ft/928m

Total 9

## Section 17

Bla Bheinn (Blaven)   3044ft/928m
Sgurr nan Gillean   3167ft/965m
Bruach na Frithe   3143ft/958m
Sgurr a'Ghreadaidh   3197ft/973m
Sgurr na Banachdich   3167ft/965m
Sgurr Dearg – Inaccessible Pinnacle   3254ft/986m
Sgurr Alasdair   3309ft/993m
Sgurr Dubh Mor   3089ft/944m
Sgurr nan Eag   3037ft/924m
Ben More (Mull)   3169ft/966m

Total 10


## Munros not having 250ft of ascent on all sides (1984-90 Revised lists)

### Section 5
Stob Coire an Laoigh   3657ft/1115m

### Section 6
Carn Sgulain   3015ft/920m

### Section 8
Carn Gluasaid   3140ft/957m

### Section 16
Creag Leacach   3238ft/987m
Carn an Tuirc   3340ft/1019m
Tom Buidhe   3140ft/957m
Tolmount   3143ft/958m
Broad Cairn (Carn Braghaid)   3268ft/998m

### Section 17
Am Basteir   3069ft/935m
Sgurr a'Mhadaidh   3012ft/918m
Sgurr Mhic Choinnich   3111ft/948m

Total 11

# Appendix B

| Stob Garbh | 3148ft/959m |
|---|---|

Rough peak

Distance_____ Miles/Km  Height_____ ft/m  Date____/____/____

Weather _____

Companions _____

Route _____

and Notes _____

_____

_____

_____

_____

_____

_____

_____

_____

## Meall na Dige                             3140ft/966m

The round hill of the ditch

Distance_____ Miles/Km   Height_____ ft/m   Date\_\_\_/\_\_\_/\_\_\_

Weather

Companions

Route

and Notes

## An Stuc                                   3643ft/1118m

The steep rock

Distance_____ Miles/Km   Height_____ ft/m   Date\_\_\_/\_\_\_/\_\_\_

Weather

Companions

Route

and Notes

190

## Beinn nan Eachan                                    3265ft/995m
### The mountain of horses

Distance_____ Miles/Km   Height_____ ft/m   Date____/____/____

Weather _____

Companions _____

Route _____

and Notes _____

_____

_____

_____

_____

_____

_____

_____


## Beinn Cheathaich                                    3076ft/937m
### The mountain of mists

Distance_____ Miles/Km   Height_____ ft/m   Date____/____/____

Weather _____

Companions _____

Route _____

and Notes _____

_____

_____

_____

_____

_____

_____

_____

## Meall Cuanail                                          3004ft/916m

Seaward looking hill, or hill of the flocks

Distance_____ Miles/Km   Height_____ ft/m   Date___/___/___

Weather _____

Companions _____

Route _____

and Notes _____

_____

_____

_____

_____

_____

_____

_____

_____


## Stob Dearg (Taynuilt Peak)                             3611ft/1101m

Red peak

Distance_____ Miles/Km   Height_____ ft/m   Date___/___/___

Weather _____

Companions _____

Route _____

and Notes _____

_____

_____

_____

_____

_____

_____

_____

## Buachaille Etive Beag – Stob Coire Raineach    3029ft/924m

The little herdsman of Etive – Peak of the corrie of the ferns

Distance_____ Miles/Km   Height_____ ft/m   Date\_\_\_/\_\_\_/\_\_\_

Weather _____

Companions _____

Route _____

and Notes _____

_____

_____

_____

_____

_____

_____

_____

## Buachaille Etive Mor – Stob na Doire    3316ft/1011m

The big herdsman of Etive – Peak of the copse

Distance_____ Miles/Km   Height_____ ft/m   Date\_\_\_/\_\_\_/\_\_\_

Weather _____

Companions _____

Route _____

and Notes _____

_____

_____

_____

_____

_____

_____

_____

## Buachaille Etive Mor – Stob na Broige      3120ft/955m

The big herdsman of Etive – Peak of the shoe

Distance_____ Miles/Km   Height_____ ft/m   Date____/____/____

Weather    _____

Companions   _____

Route    _____

and Notes    _____

_____

_____

_____

_____

_____

_____

_____

_____


## Bidean nam Bian – Stob Coire nan Lochan      3657ft/1115m

Pinnacle of the hides – Peak of the corrie of the lochans

Distance_____ Miles/Km   Height_____ ft/m   Date____/____/____

Weather    _____

Companions   _____

Route    _____

and Notes    _____

_____

_____

_____

_____

_____

_____

_____

194

## Bidean nam Bian – Stob Coire Sgreamhach                    3497ft/1070m

Pinnacle of the hides – Point of the dreadful corrie

Distance_____ Miles/Km   Height_____ ft/m   Date___/___/___

Weather   _____

Companions   _____

Route   _____

and Notes   _____

_____

_____

_____

_____

_____

_____

_____


## Stob an Fhuarain                                          3160ft/968m

Peak of the well

Distance_____ Miles/Km   Height_____ ft/m   Date___/___/___

Weather   _____

Companions   _____

Route   _____

and Notes   _____

_____

_____

_____

_____

_____

_____

_____

## Sgor Choinnich                                    3040ft/929m

Mossy peak

Distance_____ Miles/Km  Height_____ ft/m  Date___/___/___

Weather      _____

Companions   _____

Route        _____

and Notes    _____

_____

_____

_____

_____

_____

_____

_____

_____


## Gaor Bheinn (Gulvain) (South top)              3155ft/962m

Thrill, or filthy mountain

Distance_____ Miles/Km  Height_____ ft/m  Date___/___/___

Weather      _____

Companions   _____

Route        _____

and Notes    _____

_____

_____

_____

_____

_____

_____

_____

## Sgurr nan Saighead                                    3050ft/929m
The peak of the arrows

Distance_____ Miles/Km   Height_____ ft/m   Date____/____/____

Weather         _____

Companions    _____

Route           _____

and Notes      _____

_____

_____

_____

_____

_____

_____

_____


## Sgurr na Carnach                                      3270ft/1002m
The peak of the stony place

Distance_____ Miles/Km   Height_____ ft/m   Date____/____/____

Weather         _____

Companions    _____

Route           _____

and Notes      _____

_____

_____

_____

_____

_____

_____

_____

197

## Mullach na Dheiragain – Carn na Con Dhu          3176ft/968m

The redder round hill – Cairn of the black dog

Distance_____ Miles/Km   Height_____ ft/m   Date___/___/___

Weather _____

Companions _____

Route _____

and Notes _____

_____

_____

_____

_____

_____

_____

_____


## Sgurr na Lapaich          3401ft/1036m

The peak of the bog

Distance_____ Miles/Km   Height_____ ft/m   Date___/___/___

Weather _____

Companions _____

Route _____

and Notes _____

_____

_____

_____

_____

_____

_____

_____

198

## Creag Dubh  3102ft/946m

The black rock

Distance_____ Miles/Km  Height_____ ft/m  Date___/___/___

Weather _____

Companions _____

Route _____

and Notes _____

_____

_____

_____

_____

_____

_____

_____


## Creag Ghorm a'Bhealaich  3378ft/1030m

The blue rock of the pass

Distance_____ Miles/Km  Height_____ ft/m  Date___/___/___

Weather _____

Companions _____

Route _____

and Notes _____

_____

_____

_____

_____

_____

_____

_____

## Bidean an Eoin Deirg | 3430ft/1046m

The peak of the red bird

Distance_____ Miles/Km   Height_____ ft/m   Date____/____/____

Weather _____

Companions _____

Route _____

and Notes _____

_____

_____

_____

_____

_____

_____

_____

_____

## Beinn Alligin – Tom na Gruagaich | 3024ft/922m

The mountain of beauty or jewel mountain – The maidens hillock

Distance_____ Miles/Km   Height_____ ft/m   Date____/____/____

Weather _____

Companions _____

Route _____

and Notes _____

_____

_____

_____

_____

_____

_____

_____

## Beinn Eighe – Sail Mhor
### 3217ft/981m

The mountain of ice or mountain of the file – The big heel

Distance_____ Miles/Km   Height_____ ft/m   Date____/____/____

Weather   _____

Companions _____

Route   _____

and Notes   _____

_____

_____

_____

_____

_____

_____

_____


## Beinn Eighe – A'Choinneach Mhor
### 3130ft/954m

The mountain of ice or mountain of the file – The big moss

Distance_____ Miles/Km   Height_____ ft/m   Date____/____/____

Weather   _____

Companions _____

Route   _____

and Notes   _____

_____

_____

_____

_____

_____

_____

## Beinn Eighe – Spidean Coire nan Clach          3188ft/972m

The mountain of the file – The peak of the stony corrie

Distance_____ Miles/Km   Height_____ ft/m   Date\_\_\_/\_\_\_/\_\_\_

Weather _____

Companions _____

Route _____

and Notes _____

---
---
---
---
---
---
---
---

## Beinn Eighe – Sgurr an Fhir Duibhe          3160ft/963m

The mountain of the file – The peak of the black men

Distance_____ Miles/Km   Height_____ ft/m   Date\_\_\_/\_\_\_/\_\_\_

Weather _____

Companions _____

Route _____

and Notes _____

## Liathach – Stuc a'Choire Dhuibh Bhig                 2995ft/915m

The grey one – Peak of the little black corrie

Distance_____ Miles/Km   Height_____ ft/m   Date____/____/____

Weather        _____

Companions   _____

Route           _____

and Notes     _____

_____

_____

_____

_____

_____

_____

_____


## An Teallach – Stob Cadha Gobhlach               3148ft/960m

The forge – The point of the forked peak

Distance_____ Miles/Km   Height_____ ft/m   Date____/____/____

Weather        _____

Companions   _____

Route           _____

and Notes     _____

_____

_____

_____

_____

_____

_____

_____

## An Teallach – Glas Mheall Mhor                                         3217ft/981m
The forge – The big green hill

Distance_____ Miles/Km   Height_____ ft/m   Date___/___/___

Weather _____

Companions _____

Route _____

and Notes _____

_____

_____

_____

_____

_____

_____

_____


## An Teallach – Sgurr Creag an Eich                                      3335ft/1017m
The forge – The peak of the horses

Distance_____ Miles/Km   Height_____ ft/m   Date___/___/___

Weather _____

Companions _____

Route _____

and Notes _____

_____

_____

_____

_____

_____

_____

_____

## Ben Wyvis – Tom a'Choinnich                    3134ft/955m

The noble or awesome mountain – The mossy hillock

Distance_____ Miles/Km   Height_____ ft/m   Date____/____/____

Weather      _____

Companions   _____

Route        _____

and Notes    _____

_____

_____

_____

_____

_____

_____

_____


## Ben Wyvis – Glas Leathad Beag                    3044ft/928m

The noble or awesome mountain – The little green grassy slope

Distance_____ Miles/Km   Height_____ ft/m   Date____/____/____

Weather      _____

Companions   _____

Route        _____

and Notes    _____

_____

_____

_____

_____

_____

_____

_____

## Cairn Gorm – Cairn Lochan                                      3983ft/1215m
Blue mountain – Tarn hill

Distance_____ Miles/Km   Height_____ ft/m   Date____/____/____

Weather        _____

Companions    _____

Route          _____

and Notes      _____

_____

_____

_____

_____

_____

_____

_____

_____


## Cairn Toul – Sgor an Lochain Uaine                             4150ft/1258m
Hill of the barn – Peak of the green tarn

Distance_____ Miles/Km   Height_____ ft/m   Date____/____/____

Weather        _____

Companions    _____

Route          _____

and Notes      _____

_____

_____

_____

_____

_____

_____

_____

_____

| **Mam nan Carn** | **3224ft/986m** |
|---|---|

Round hill of the stony hillside

Distance_____ Miles/Km   Height_____ ft/m   Date____/____/____

Weather       _____

Companions  _____

Route          _____

and Notes    _____

_____

_____

_____

_____

_____

_____

_____

| **Beinn Iutharn Bheag** | **3121ft/953m** |
|---|---|

Little Hell's peak

Distance_____ Miles/Km   Height_____ ft/m   Date____/____/____

Weather       _____

Companions  _____

Route          _____

and Notes    _____

_____

_____

_____

_____

_____

_____

_____

# Appendix C

## 3000ft PEAKS WITH 250ft OF REASCENT ON ALL SIDES NOT LISTED IN MUNRO'S TABLES 1980-1990

### SECTION 1

**Stob Garbh    3148ft/959m**
Metric height from 1:25 000 map.
Col to Cruach Ardrain between 850-860m.
Reascent from Cruach Ardrain side 99m-109m or between 324ft and 357ft.

**Meall na Dige    3140ft/966m**
Metric height from 1:25 000 map.
Col to Stob Coire an Lochain/Stob Binnein between 880-890m.
Large area within 880m contour suggests height nearer lower elevation.
Reascent from Stob Coire an Lochain side 76m-86m or between 249ft and 282ft (Large area within 76m contour suggests reascent nearer 282ft than 249ft)

### SECTION 3

**An Stur +    3643ft/1118m**
Metric height from 1:25 000 map.
Col to Meall Greigh between spot height 991m.
Col to Ben Lawers (Bealach Dubh) 920m-930m (spot height at 942m is a small knob).
Reascent from Meall Greigh side 127m or 416ft.
Reascent from Ben Lawers side 188m-198m or between 616ft and 649ft.

**Beinn nan Eachan    3265ft/995m**
Metric height from 1:50 000 map (1:25 000 map gives cairn in 1000m contour).
Col to Meall Garbh/Meall nan Tarmachan between 900m-910m.
Reascent from Meall Garbh side 85m-95m or between 278ft and 311ft.

**Beinn Cheathaich    3076ft/937m**
Metric height from 1:50 000 map
Crest to Meall Glas 850m-860m.
Col to Meall a'Churain (Lairig a'Churain) 609m.
Reascent from Meall Glas side 77m-87m or between 252ft and 285ft.
Reascent from Lairig a'Chuarain 328m or 1076ft.

208

+ Reclassified as mountain in the *Munro's Tables* of 1997.

## SECTION 4

**Stob Dearg (Taynuilt Peak)   3611ft/1104m**
Metric height from 1:25 000 map.
Col to Ben Cruachan 1000m-1010m.
Reascent from Ben Cruachan side 94m-104m or between 308ft and 341ft.

**Meall Cuanail   3004ft/918m**
Imperial height from 1″ map.
Metric height from 1:25 000 map.
Col to Ben Cruachan (Bealach an Lochain) 820m-830m.
Reascent from Ben Cruachan side 88m-98m or between 288ft and 321ft.

**Buachaille Etive Beag - Stob Coire Raineach +   3029ft/925m**
Metric height from 1:25 000 map.
Col at centre of ridge (Mam Buidhe) spot height at 748m.
Reascent from Mam Buidhe 177m or 580ft.

**Buachaille Etive Mor – Stob na Doire   3316ft/1011m**
Metric height from 1:50 000 map.
Col to Stob Dearg 870m-880m.
Col to Stob Coire Altruim/Stob na Broige 830m-840m.
Reascent from Stob Dearg side 131m-141m or between 429ft and 462ft.
Reascent from Stob na Broige side 171m-181m or between 561ft and 593ft.
Pre-metric 1:25 000 map gives summit at 3316ft.
Col to Stob Dearg (Head of Coire na Tulaich) 2850ft-2875ft.
Col to Stob Coire Altruim 2675ft-2700ft.
Reascent from Stob Dearg side 441ft-466ft.
Reascent from Stob Coire Altruim side 616ft-641ft.

**Buachaille Etive Mor - Stob na Broige +   3120ft/956m**
Height from 1:25 000 map.
Col to Stob na Doire 830m-840m.
Reascent from Stob na Doire side 116m-126m or between 380ft and 413ft.

**Bidean nam Bian – Stob Coire nan Lochan   3657ft/1115m**
Height from 1:25 000 map.
Col to Bidean nam Bian summit 990m-1000m.
Reascent from Bidean nam Bian side 115m-125m or between 377ft and 410ft.

**Bidean nam Bian - Stob Coire Sgreamhach +   3497ft/1072**
Metric height from 1:25 000 map.
Col to Bidean nam Bian (Bealach Dearg) spot height at 944m.
Reascent from Bealach Dearg 128m or 419ft.

+ Reclassified as mountain in the *Munro's Tables* of 1997.

**Stob an Fhuarain   3160ft/968m**
Imperial height from 6″ map contour (Munro's Tables 1974).
Munro's Tables show 6″ map at 3160ft approx.
Metric height from 1:25 000 map.
Crest to Sgor na h-Ulaidh 860m-870m.
Reascent from Sgor na h-Ulaidh 98m-108m or between 321ft and 354ft.

## SECTION 5

**Sgor Choinnich   3040ft/929m**
Metric height from 1:25 000 map.
Col to Sgor Gaibhre (Bealach nan Sgor) spot height 802m.
Reascent from Bealach nan Sgor 127m or 416ft.
\* An original Munro.

## SECTION 7

**Gaor Bheinn (Gulvain) (South top)   3155ft/962m**
Imperial height from 1″ map.
Metric height from 1:25 000 map.
Crest at centre of summit ridge at 860m-870m.
Reascent from north top side 92m-102m or between 301ft and 334ft.

## SECTION 8

**Sgurr nan Saighead 3050ft/929m**
Metric height from 1:25 000 map.
Col to Sgurr Fhuaran (Bealach Buidhe) 820-830m.
Reascent from Bealach Buidhe between 99m and 109m or between 324ft and 357ft.

**Sgurr na Carnach +   3270ft/1002m**
Metric height from 1:25 000 map.
Col to Sgurr Fhuaran (Bealach na Carnach) 860m-870m.
Col to Sgurr na Ciste Duibhe (Bealach na Craoibhe) 840m-850m.
Reascent from Bealach na Carnach between 132m and 142m or between 433ft and 465ft.
Reascent from Bealach na Craoibhe between 152m and 162m or between 498ft and 531ft.

**Mullach na Dheiragain (Carn na Con Dhu)   3176ft/967m**
Metric height from 1:25 000 map.
Col to Sgurr na Ceathreamhnan (Bealach nan Daoine) 830m-840m.
Col to Mullach na Dheiragain (Bealach na Con Dhu) 880m-890m.
Reascent from Bealach nan Daoine 127m-137m or between 416ft and 449ft.
Reascent from Bealach na Con Dhu 77m-87m or between 252ft and 285ft.

+ Reclassified as mountain in the *Munro's Tables* of 1997.

**Sgurr na Lapaich   3401ft/1036m**
Metric height from 1:25 000 map.
Col to Mam Sodhail above Cos Raineach 920m-930m.
Reascent from col above Cos Raineach 106m-116m or between 347ft and 380ft.
\* An original Munro.

## SECTION 9

**Creag Dubh   3102ft/946m**
Metric height from Munro's Tables 1990.
Col to Carn nan Gobhar 840m-850m (just a marginal split between 850m contours meeting at the col).
Reascent from Carn nan Gobhar 96m-106m or between 314ft and 347ft (closer to 314ft but certainly exceeding 250ft).
1:50 000 map gives summit in 940m contour.
Reascent from Carn nan Gobhar side 90m-100m or between 295ft and 320ft.
1:25 000 map (direct update from old 1″) gives col at just below 853m contour.
Reascent from Sgurr na Lapaich side minimum 93m or 305ft.
Contour ring count gives fully 300ft of reascent.
\* An original Munro.

**Creag Ghorm a'Bhealaich   3380ft/1030m**
Metric height from 1:50 000 map.
Col to Sgurr Fhuar-thuill 940m-950m.
Col to Sgurr a'Choire Ghlais 900m-910m.
Reascent from Sgurr Fhuar-thuill side 80m-90m or between 262ft and 295ft.
Reascent from Sgurr a'Choire Ghlais side 120m-130m or between 393ft and 426ft.
Pre-metric 1:25 000 map.
Col to Sgurr Fhuar-thuill spot height at 3115ft.
Col to Sgurr a'Choire Ghlais (Bealach Toll Sgaile) between 2950ft and 2975ft.
Reascent from Sgurr Fhuar-thuill side 265ft.
Reascent from Bealach Toll Sgaile between 405ft and 430ft.

**Bidean an Eoin Deirg   3430ft/1046m**
Metric height from 1:25 000 map.
Col to Sgurr a'Chaorachain 960m-970m (1:50 000 map).
N.B. Broken 960m contour.
Reascent from Sgurr a'Chaorachain side 76m-86m or between 249ft-282ft.
Col to Sgurr a'Chaorachain between 25ft-50ft below 975m contour ring (1:25 000 map direct update from old 1″ map).
Col at 3148ft-3173ft, or 959m-967m.
Summit at 1046m or 3431ft.
Reascent from Sgurr a'Chaorachain side 258ft-283ft.
Reascent by metric measurement 79m-87m or between 259ft and 285ft.
\* An original Munro.

## SECTION 10
**Beinn Alligin - Tom na Gruagaich +  3024ft/922m**
Metric height from 1:25 000 map (Outdoor Leisure 8)
Col to Sgurr Mhor spot height at 767m.
Reascent from Sgurr Mhor side 155m or 508ft.

**Beinn Eighe – Sail Mhor  3217ft/980m**
Metric height from 1:25 000 map (Outdoor Leisure 8).
Col to A'Choinneach Mhor 850m-860m (1:50 000 map).
Reascent from A'Choinneach Mhor side 121m-131m or between 396ft and 429ft.
Contour ring count on 1:25 000 map gives 375ft.
Col to A'Choinneach Mhor 860m-870m (1:25 000 map Outdoor Leisure 8).
Reascent from A'Choinneach Mhor 110m-120m or between 360ft and 393ft.

**Beinn Eighe – A'Choinneach Mhor 3130ft/975m**
Metric height from Munro's Tables 1990 (975c).
1:25 000 map gives 975 contour ring at western end of summit.
1:50 000 map gives 970m contour at summit.
1:10 000 map gives 953m contour ring at eastern end.
Col to Sail Mhor 850m-860m (1:50 000 map).
Col to Ruadh-stac Mor 870m-880m (1:50 000 map).
Col to Ruadh-stac Mor 853 + 50ft-75ft (contour count) 2838ft-2873ft (1:25 000 map).
Col to Spidean Coire nan Clach spot height at 821m (1:25 000 map).
Reascent from Sail Mhor side to summit (at 970m) 110m-120m or between 360ft and 393ft.
Reascent from Ruadh-stac Mor side to summit (at 970m) 90m-100m or between 295ft and 328ft.
Reascent from Spidean Coire nan Clach side to summit (at 970m) 149m or 488ft.
Reascent from Sail Mhor to summit (at 975m) 115m-125m or between 377ft and 410ft.
Reascent from Ruadh-stac Mor side to summit (at 975m) 95m-105m or between 311ft and 344ft.
Contour ring count on 1:25 000 map on reascent from Sail Mhor side gives 275ft+.
Contour ring count on 1:25 000 map on reascent from Ruadh-stac Mor side gives 350ft.
Reascent from Spidean Coire nan Clach side to summit (at 975m) 154m or 505ft.

+ Reclassified as mountain in the *Munro's Tables* of 1997.

Col to Sail Mhor 860m-870m (1:25 000 Outdoor Leisure 8).
Col to Ruadh-stac Mor spot height 868m (1:25 000 Outdoor Leisure 8).
Col to Spidean Coire nan Clach 820m-830m.
Reascent from Sail Mhor side 106m-116m or between 347ft and 380ft.
Reascent from Ruadh-stac Mor side 108m or 354ft.
Reascent from Stob Coire nan Clach side 146m-156m or between 478ft and 511ft.

**Beinn Eighe - Spidean Coire nan Clach +   3188ft/972m**
Metric height from 1:25 000 map.
Metric height from 1:25 000 map (Outdoor Leisure 8) 977m.
Col to A'Choinneach Mhor spot height at 821m.
Col to Sgurr an Fhir Duibhe 823m (2700ft) + 50ft-75ft (additional contours at intervals of 25ft) gives col at 2750-2775ft (838m-845m).
Reascent from A'Choinneach Mhor side 151m or 495ft.
Reascent from Sgurr an Fhir Duibhe side 127m-134m or between 416ft and 439ft.
Contour count on reascent from Sgurr an Fhir Duibhe side gives 400ft.
Col to A'Choinneach Mhor 820m-830m (1:25 000 map Outdoor Leisure 8).
Col to Sgurr nan Fhir Duibhe 840m-850m (1:25 000 map Outdoor Leisure 8).
Reascent from A'Choinneach Mhor 142m-152m or between 465ft and 498ft.
Reascent from Sgurr nan Fhir Duibhe side 122m-132m or between 465ft and 498ft.

**Beinn Eighe – Sgurr an Fhir Duibhe   3160ft/963m**
Metric height from 1:25 000 map (Outdoor Leisure 8) 963m.
Col to Spidean Coire nan Clach 838m-845m (see calculation above).
Reascent from Spidean Coire nan Clach side 118m-125m or between 387ft and 410ft.
Contour count on reascent from Spidean Coire nan Clach side gives 350ft+.
Col to Spidean Coire nan Clach 840m-850m (1:25 000 map Outdoor Leisure 8).
Reascent from Spidean Coire nan Clach side 113m-123m or between 370ft and 403ft.

**Liathach – Stuc a'Choire Dhuibh Bhig   2995ft/915m**
Metric height from 1:25 000 Outdoor Leisure Map 8 (1986 print).
Col to Stob a'Coire Liath Mhor 830m-840m.
Reascent from Stob a'Coire Liath Mhor side 75m-85m or between 246ft and 278ft.

+ Reclassified as mountain in the *Munro's Tables* of 1997.

## SECTION 11
**An Teallach – Stob Cadha Gobhlach    3148ft/960m**
Metric height from 1:25 000 map.
Col to Sgurr Fiona (foot of Corrag Buidhe) 830m-840m.
Col to Sail Liath 890m-900m.
Reascent from foot of Corrag Buidhe 120m-130m or between 393ft or 426ft.
Reascent from Sail Liath side 60m-70m or between 196ft and 229ft (Sail Liath becomes a top of Stob Cadha Gobhlach).
Height from 1:25 000 map.
Col to Sgurr Fiona (1:25 000 pre-metric) spot height at 2733ft.
Col to Sail Liath (1:25 000 pre-metric) spot height at 2949ft.
Reascent from foot of Corrag Buidhe 415ft.
Reascent from Sail Liath side 199ft.


**An Teallach – Glas Mheall Mhor    3217ft/979m**
Imperial and Metric heights from 1:25 000 maps.
Col to Bidein a'Ghlas Thuill 2875ft-2900ft.
Reascent from Bidein a'Ghlas Thuill side 317ft-342ft.
Col to Bidein a'Ghlas Thuill 890m-900m.
Reascent from Bidein a'Ghlas Thuill side 87m-88m or between 324ft and 357ft.


**An Teallach – Sgurr Creag an Eich    3335ft/1017m**
Imperial and Metric heights from 1:25 000 maps.
Col to Sgurr Fiona spot height at 3024ft.
Reascent from Sgurr Fiona side 311ft.
Col to Sgurr Fiona spot height not quantified 920m-930m.
Reascent from Sgurr Fiona side 87m-97m or between 285ft and 318ft.


**Ben Wyvis – Tom a'Choinnich    3134ft/953m**
Metric height from 1:25 000 map.
Col to Glas Leathad Mor (Bealach Tom a'Choinnich 860m-870m.
Col to Glas Leathad Beag spot height at 796m.
Reascent from Glas Leathad Mor side 83m-93m or between 272ft and 305ft.
Reascent from Glas Leathad Beag side 157m or 515ft.


**Ben Wyvis – Glas Leathad Beag    3044ft/928m**
Metric height from 1:25 000 map.
Col to Tom a'Choinnich spot height at 796m.
Reascent from Tom a'Choinnich side 132m or 433ft.

## SECTION 14

**Cairn Lochan    3983ft/1215m**
Metric height from 1:25 000 map.
Col to Cairn Gorm spot height 1111m to east of Fiacaill Buttress.
Col to Ben Macdui (Lochan Buidhe) spot height at 1125m.
Reascent from Cairn Gorm side 104m or 341ft.
Reascent from Ben Macdui 90m or 295ft.

**Sgor an Lochain Uaine +    4150ft/1258m**
Metric height from 1:25 000 map.
Col to Cairn Toul spot height at 1140m.
Col to Braeriach (top of Great Gully) 1120m-1130m.
Reascent from Cairn Toul side 118m or 387ft.
Reascent from Braeriach side 128m-138m or between 419ft and 452ft.
* An original Munro.

**A'Choinneach    3345ft/1017m**
Metric height from 1:25 000 map.
Col to Cairn Gorm (The Saddle) spot height at 807m.
Col to Bynack More spot height at 940m (in small contour ring).
Reascent from Cairn Gorm side 210m or 688ft.
Reascent from Bynack More side 77m or 252ft.
* Reduced to a top in 1980/1984/1990 Munro's Tables.

## SECTION 15

**Mam nan Carn    3224ft/986m**
Metric height from 1:25 000 map.
Col to Beinn Iutharn Bheag spot height at 848m.
Col to Beinn Iutharn Mhor 900m-910m (marginal dip below 910m contour).
Col to Carn an Righ spot height at 771m.
Reascent from Beinn Iutharn Bheag side 138m or 452ft.
Reascent from Beinn Iutharn Mhor side 76m-86m or between 249ft and 282ft (at 909m separation = 252ft).
Reascent from Carn an Righ side 215m or 705ft.

**Beinn Iutharn Bheag    3121ft/953m**
Metric height from 1:25 000 map.
Col to Mam nan Carn spot height at 848m.
Reascent from Mam nan Carn side 105m or 344ft.
* An original Munro.

+ Reclassified as mountain in the *Munro's Tables* of 1997.

# TOPS PROMOTED IN 1980 REVISION OF MUNRO'S TABLES (BROWN/DONALDSON)

## SECTION 5

**Sgor an Iubhair ‡   3284ft/1001m**
Metric height from 1:25 000 map.
Col to Stob Ban 760m-770m.
Col to Sgurr a'Mhaim spot height at 924m.
Col to Am Bodach 880m-890m.
Reascent from Stob Ban side 231m-241m or between 757ft and 790ft.
Reascent from Sgurr a'Mhaim side 77m or 252ft.
Reascent from Am Bodach side 111m-121m or between 364ft and 396ft.

## SECTION 7

**Garbh Chioch Mhor   3365ft/1013m**
Metric height from 1:25 000 map.
Col to Sgurr na Ciche (Feadan na Ciche) spot height at 845m.
Col to Sgurr nan Coireachan (Bealach Coire nan Gall) spot height at 733m.
Reascent from Feadan na Ciche 168m or 551ft.
Reascent from Bealach Coire nan Gall 280m or 918ft.

## SECTION 10

**Liathach – Mullach an Rathain   3358ft/1023m**
Metric height from 1:25 000 map.
Col to Am Fasarinen 880m-890m.
Reascent from Am Fasarinen side 133m-143m or between 436ft and 469ft.

## SECTION 11

**An Teallach – Sgurr Fiona   3474ft/1060m**
Metric height from 1:25 000 map.
Col to Stob Cadha Gobhlach 830m-840m.
Col to Bidein a'Ghlas Thuill 920m-930m (narrow edge in 920m contour).
Reascent from Stob Cadha Gobhlach side 220m-230m or between 721ft and 754ft.
Reascent from Bidein a'Ghlas Thuill side 130m-140m or between 426ft and 459ft.

216

‡ Demoted to Top in the *Munro's Tables* of 1997.

# MOUNTAINS DEMOTED TO TOPS IN MUNRO'S TABLES 1980 (BROWN/DONALDSON REVISION)

## SECTION 1

**Beinn an Lochain   3021ft/901m**
Metric height from 1:25 000 map.
★ Would not qualify as 3000ft mountain due to height confirmed at below 3000ft.

## SECTION 6

**Carn Ban   3087ft/942m**
Metric height from 1:50 000 map.
Col to Carn Dearg 880m-890m.
Col to Carn Ballach/Carn Sgulain (gap east of Meall a'Bhothain) 850m-860m.
Reascent from Carn Dearg side 52m-62m or between 170ft and 203ft.
Reascent from Carn Ballach/Carn Sgulain side 82m-92m or between 269ft and 301ft.
★ Would not qualify as a mountain under 250ft rule.

**Carn Ballach   3020ft/920m**
Metric height from 1:50 000 map.
Col to Carn Ban/Carn Dearg 870m-880m.
Col to Carn Sgulain (gap east of Meall a'Bhothain) 850-860m.
Reascent from Carn Ban/Carn Dearg side 40m-50m or between 131ft and 164ft.
Reascent from Carn Sgulain side 60m-70m or between 196ft and 229ft.

## SECTION 14

**A'Choinneach   3345ft/1017m**
Metric height from 1:25 000 map.
Col to Cairn Gorm (The Saddle) spot height at 807m.
Col to Bynack More spot height at 940m (in small contour ring).
Reascent from Cairn Gorm side 210m or 688ft.
Reascent from Bynack More side 77m or 252ft.
★ Would qualify as a mountain under 250ft rule.

**Carn Cloich-mhuillin   3087ft/942m**
Metric height from 1:25 000 map.
Col to Beinn Bhrotain spot height at 867m.
Reascent from Beinn Bhrotain side 75m or 246ft.
★ Would not qualify as a mountain under 250ft rule.

**Meall Dubhag    3268ft/998m**
Metric height from 1:25 000 map.
Col to Mullach Clach a'Bhlair 900m-910m.
Col to Carn Ban Mor/Sgor Gaoith spot height at 966m.
Reascent from Mullach Clach a'Bhlair side 88m-98m or between 288ft and 321ft.
Reascent from Carn Ban Mor/Sgor Gaoith side 32m or 104m.
\* Would not qualify as a mountain under 250ft rule.

**Carn Ban Mor    3443ft/1052m**
Metric height from 1:25 000 map.
Col to Meall Dubhag spot height at 966m.
Col to Sgor Gaoith spot height at 1012m.
Reascent from Meall Dubhag side 86m or 282ft.
Reascent from Sgor Gaoith side 40m or 131ft.
\* Would not qualify as a mountain under 250ft rule.

**Geal-charn    3019ft/920m**
Metric height from 1:25 000 map.
Col to Meall Buidhe spot height at 866m.
Reascent from Sgor Gaoith side 54m or 177ft.

## Note for the 2003 edition

MOUNTAIN DEMOTED TO A TOP IN *MUNRO'S TABLES* OF 1997

**Sgor an Iubhair ‡    3284ft/1001m**
Metric height from 1:25 000 map.
Col to Stob Ban 760m-770m.
Col to Sgurr a'Mhaim spot height at 924m.
Col to Am Bodach 880m-890m.
Reascent from Stob Ban side 231m-241m or between 757ft and 790ft.
Reascent from Sgurr a'Mhaim side 77m or 252ft.
Reascent from Am Bodach side 111m-121m or between 364ft and 396ft.

# HEIGHTS CLASSED AS MOUNTAINS IN MUNRO'S ORIGINAL LIST NOT ELSEWHERE RECORDED

## SECTION 3

**Beinn a'Chuirn    3030ft/923m**
Metric height from 1:25 000 map.
Col to Beinn Mhanach spot height at 849m.
Reascent from Beinn Mhanach side 74m or 242ft.
★ Would not qualify as a mountain under 250ft rule.

## SECTION 14

**Carn Eas    3556ft/1089m**
Metric height from 1:50 000 map.
Col to Ben Avon 1060m-1070m.
Reascent from Ben Avon side 19m-29m or between 62ft and 95ft (A rise at the end of a broad ridge).
★ Would not qualify as a mountain under 250ft rule.

**Creag an Dail Mhor (Creag an Dala Mhoir)    3189ft/972m**
Metric height from Munro's Tables 1990 (1:50 000 map gives 970m contour).
Col to Carn Eas 900m-910m.
Reascent from Carn Eas side 62m-72m or between 203ft and 236ft.
★ Would not qualify as a mountain under 250ft rule.

**Creag na Leth-choin (Creag na Leacainn south top)    3448ft/1053m**
Metric height from 1:25 000 map.
Col to Cairn Lochan spot height at 997m.
Reascent from Cairn Lochan side 56m or 183ft.
★ Would not qualify as a mountain under 250ft rule.

## SECTION 15

**Glas Mheall Mor    3037ft/928m**
Metric height from 1:25 000 map.
Col to A'Bhuidheanach Bheag spot height at 860m.
Reascent from A'Bhuidheanach Bheag side 68m or 223ft.
★ Would not qualify as a mountain under 250ft rule.

**Meall a'Chaorainn    3004ft/916m**
Metric height from 1:25 000 map.
Col to A'Bhuidheanach Bheag 900m-910m.
Reascent from A'Bhuidheanach Bheag side 6m-16m or between 19ft and 52ft.
(A lump at the end of the nose of A'Bhuidheanach Bheag).
★ Would not qualify as a mountain under 250ft rule.

**Carn Bhinnein    3006ft/917m**
Metric height from 1:25 000 map.
Col to Carn a'Gheoidh spot height 854m.
Reascent from Carn a'Gheoidh side 63m or 206ft.
★ Would not qualify as a mountain under 250ft rule.

## MOUNTAINS LISTED IN MUNRO'S TABLES 1980-1990 WHICH FAIL TO QUALIFY UNDER 250ft RULE

### SECTION 5
**Stob Coire an Laoigh  3657ft/1116m**
Imperial height from 6″ map.
Metric height from 1:25 000 map.
Col to Sgurr Choinnich Mor 930m-940m.
Crest to Stob Choire Claurigh spot height at 1055m (1:25 000 map) immediately east of Stob Coire an Laoigh.
Crest to Stob Choire Claurigh (between Stob Coire Cath na Sine and Stob a'Choire Leith) 1040m-1050m.
Reascent from Sgurr Choinnich Mor side 176m-186m or between 577ft and 610ft.
Reascent from Stob Choire Claurigh side (by spot height) 61m or 200ft.
Reascent from Stob Choire Claurigh side (crest between Stob Coire Cath na Sine and Stob a'Choire Leith) 66m-76m or between 216ft and 249ft.

### SECTION 6
**Carn Sgulain 3015ft/920m**
Imperial height from 1″ map.
Metric height from 1:50 000 map.
Depression in plateau towards Carn Ballach (East of Meall a' Bhrotain) 850m-860m.
Depression in plateau towards A'Chailleach (Allt Cuil na Caillich) 810m-820m.
Reascent from Carn Ballach side 60m-70m or between 196ft and 229ft.
Reascent from A'Chailleach side 100m-110m or between 328ft and 360ft.

### SECTION 8
**Carn Ghluasaid  3140ft/957m**
Metric height from 1:25 000 map.
Col to Sgurr nan Conbhairean spot height at 895m.
Reascent from Glas Bhealach 62m or 203ft.

### SECTION 16
**Creag Leacach  3238ft/987m**
Metric height from 1:25 000 map.
Col to Glas Maol spot height at 933m.
Reascent from Glas Maol side 54m or 177ft.

**Carn an Tuirc  3340ft/1019m**
Metric height from 1:25 000 map.
Col to Cairn of Claise 950m-960m.
Reascent from Cairn of Claise side 59m-69m or between 193ft and 226ft.

**Tom Buidhe   3140ft/957m**
Imperial height from 1″ map.
Metric height from 1:25 000 map.
Plateau on Mayar ridge 817m (Red Burn – Burn of Fialzioch depression) (1:25 000 map).
Depression to west leading to Cairn of Claise 886m spot height (common to Tolmount).
Reascent from Mayar side 140m or 459ft.
Reascent from Cairn of Claise/Tolmount side 71m or 232ft.

**Tolmount   3143ft/958m**
Imperial height from 1″ map.
Metric height from 1:25 000 map.
Depression leading to Cairn of Claise/Tom Buidhe 886m spot height (1:25 000 map).
Depression leading to Crow Craigies/Jock's Road path 874m spot height (1:25 000 map).
Reascent from Cairn of Claise/Tom Buidhe side 72m or 236ft.
Reascent from Jock's Road path side 84m or 275ft.

**Broad Cairn   3268ft/998m**
Metric height from 1:25 000 map.
Col to Cairn Bannoch spot height at 934m.
Reascent from Cairn Bannoch side 64m or 209ft.

## SECTION 17

**Am Basteir 3069ft/935m**
Metric height from 1:25 000 map.
Pre-metric data from S.M.C. "The Island of Skye" guide.
Col to Sgurr nan Gillean (Bealach a'Bhasteir) 2733ft/2780ft.
Col to Bruach na Frithe (Bealach nan Lice) 2940ft approx.
Reascent from Bealach a'Bhasteir 289ft/336ft.
Reascent from Bealach nan Lice 129ft (approx).
1:50 000 map gives 870m (2854ft) contour on north side of Bealach nan Lice.
Reascent from Bealach nan Lice 65m (approx) or 213ft.


**Sgurr a'Mhadaidh 3012ft/918m**
Imperial height from S.M.C. guide.
Metric height from 1:25 000 map (Outdoor Leisure 8).
Col at Bealach na Glaic Mhoire 2492ft (S.M.C. guide).
Col at An Dorus 2779ft (S.M.C. guide).
Reascent from Bealach na Glaic Mhoire 520ft.
Reascent from An Dorus 233ft.


**Sgurr Mhic Choinnich 3111ft/948m**
Imperial height from S.M.C guide.
Metric height from Munro's Tables 1990.
Col at Bealach Coire Lagan 2690ft (S.M.C. guide).
Col at Bealach Mhic Coinnich 2928ft (S.M.C. guide).
Reascent from Bealach Coire Lagan 421ft.
Reascent from Beallach Mhic Coinnich 183ft.

**Furth of Scotland**

Mountains over 3000ft outwith Scotland have been referred to by Munroists north of the border as a group "Furth of Scotland", a term coined by Eric Maxwell of the Grampian Club in Dundee.

The term "Munro" as applied to hills outside Scotland is incorrect as they were not subject to Munro's attentions.

The English and Welsh peaks are not classified as "mountains" and "tops" in the Munro idiom, possibly because they are so few in number.

In England there are seven peaks, of which four are generally regarded as mountains. Wales possesses fifteen summits above 3000ft, and were 250ft of ascent on all sides to be adopted as the criteria for establishing "mountain" status, eight of the Welsh peaks would qualify. The Irish peaks over 3000ft have been classified in a similar manner to that adopted in Scotland, and of the thirteen summits over 3000ft seven are classified as mountains.

**Furth of Scotland 3000ft mountains (with 250ft of ascent on all sides)**

**England**
Scafell   3162ft/964m
Scafell Pike   3206ft/977m
Skiddaw (Skiddaw Man)   3054ft/931m
Helvellyn   3116ft/950m

**Wales**
Snowdon – Yr Wyddfa   3560ft/1085m
Tryfan   3010ft/915m
Glyder Fawr   3279ft/999m
Y Garn   3104ft/947m
Elidir Fawr   3030ft/923m
Carnedd Dafydd   3427ft/1044m
Carnedd Llewelyn   3485ft/1064m
Foel-fras   3092ft/942m

**Ireland**
Lugnaquillia   3039ft/927m
Galtymore   3018ft/920m
Macgillycuddy's Reeks – Cummeennapeasta   3191ft/972m
                                – Carrauntoohil   3414ft/1039m
                                – Caher   3250ft/990m
                                – Beenkeragh   3314ft/1010m
Brandon Mountain   3127ft/953m

# England

*Scafell Pike and Scafell*

## Scafell                                                    3162ft/964m

Distance_____ Miles/Km   Height_____ ft/m   Date___/___/___
Weather        _____
Companions   _____
Route          _____
and Notes    _____

_____
_____
_____
_____
_____
_____
_____
_____

## Scafell Pike                                              3206ft/977m

Distance_____ Miles/Km   Height_____ ft/m   Date___/___/___
Weather        _____
Companions   _____
Route          _____
and Notes    _____

_____
_____
_____
_____
_____
_____
_____

| Skiddaw or Skiddaw Man | 3054ft/931m |

Distance_____ Miles/Km   Height_____ ft/m   Date____/____/____
Weather        _____
Companions     _____
Route          _____
and Notes      _____

_____
_____
_____
_____
_____
_____
_____
_____
_____

| Helvellyn | 3116ft/950m |

Distance_____ Miles/Km   Height_____ ft/m   Date____/____/____
Weather        _____
Companions     _____
Route          _____
and Notes      _____

_____
_____
_____
_____
_____
_____
_____
_____

# *Wales*

*Yr Wyddfa and Crib-goch*

228

## Snowdon – Yr Wyddfa                    3560ft/1085m

The tumulus or burial mound

Distance_____ Miles/Km   Height_____ ft/m   Date___/___/___

Weather _____

Companions _____

Route _____

and Notes _____

_____

_____

_____

_____

_____

_____

_____

_____


## Tryfan                    3010ft/915m

The three beacons; very steep, high mountain or one with a sharp or finger-like summit

Distance_____ Miles/Km   Height_____ ft/m   Date___/___/___

Weather _____

Companions _____

Route _____

and Notes _____

_____

_____

_____

_____

_____

_____

_____

## Glyder Fawr                                              3279ft/999m

The big heap or cairn

Distance_____ Miles/Km   Height_____ ft/m   Date___/___/___

Weather      _____

Companions   _____

Route        _____

and Notes    _____

_____

_____

_____

_____

_____

_____

_____


## Y Garn                                                   3104ft/947m

The eminence or rock

Distance_____ Miles/Km   Height_____ ft/m   Date___/___/___

Weather      _____

Companions   _____

Route        _____

and Notes    _____

_____

_____

_____

_____

_____

_____

_____

## Elidir Fawr                                                    3030ft/923m

Big or greater Elidir

Distance_____ Miles/Km   Height_____ ft/m   Date___/___/___

Weather         _____

Companions      _____

Route           _____

and Notes       _____

_____

_____

_____

_____

_____

_____

_____


## Carnedd Dafydd                                                3427ft/1044m

David's cairn

Distance_____ Miles/Km   Height_____ ft/m   Date___/___/___

Weather         _____

Companions      _____

Route           _____

and Notes       _____

_____

_____

_____

_____

_____

_____

| Carnedd Llewelyn | 3485ft/1064m |
|---|---|

Llewelyn's cairn

Distance_____ Miles/Km   Height_____ ft/m   Date___/___/___

Weather _____

Companions _____

Route _____

and Notes _____

_____

_____

_____

_____

_____

_____

_____

_____


| Foel-fras | 3092ft/942m |
|---|---|

The fat hill

Distance_____ Miles/Km   Height_____ ft/m   Date___/___/___

Weather _____

Companions _____

Route _____

and Notes _____

_____

_____

_____

_____

_____

_____

_____

# Ireland

*Carrantooil and Beenkeragh*

## Lugnaquillia                                 3039ft/927m

Hollow of the woods

Distance_____ Miles/Km   Height_____ ft/m   Date___/___/___

Weather _____

Companions _____

Route _____

and Notes _____

_____

_____

_____

_____

_____

_____

_____

## Galtymore                                   3018ft/920m

Big mountain of the woods

Distance_____ Miles/Km   Height_____ ft/m   Date___/___/___

Weather _____

Companions _____

Route _____

and Notes _____

_____

_____

_____

_____

_____

_____

234

## Cummeennapeasta                                      3191ft/972m
Hollow of the serpent

Distance_____ Miles/Km   Height_____ ft/m   Date____/____/____

Weather      _____

Companions   _____

Route        _____

and Notes    _____

_____

_____

_____

_____

_____

_____

_____


## Carrauntoohil                                        3414ft/1039m
Inverted reaping hook

Distance_____ Miles/Km   Height_____ ft/m   Date____/____/____

Weather      _____

Companions   _____

Route        _____

and Notes    _____

_____

_____

_____

_____

_____

_____

_____

## Caher                                                      3250ft/990m
Fort

Distance_____ Miles/Km   Height_____ ft/m   Date____/____/____

Weather      _____

Companions   _____

Route        _____

and Notes    _____

_____

_____

_____

_____

_____

_____

_____

_____


## Beenkeragh                                                3314ft/1010m
Black peak or peak of the sheep

Distance_____ Miles/Km   Height_____ ft/m   Date____/____/____

Weather      _____

Companions   _____

Route        _____

and Notes    _____

_____

_____

_____

_____

_____

_____

_____

## Brandon Mountain · 3127ft/953m

St. Brendan's mountain

Distance_____ Miles/Km   Height_____ ft/m   Date____/____/____

Weather _____

Companions _____

Route _____

and Notes _____

_____

_____

_____

_____

_____

_____

_____

_____

On the summit of Brandon Mountain there are the remains of an oratory dedicated to St. Brendan the navigator. He is reputed to have sought out the summit for reflection before setting out with fellow monks in frail curraghs for the coasts of Greenland and America. The Saint's Road, the path up from Ballybrack, is said to be named after him.

# Summary of mountains with 250ft of ascent on all sides

**Scotland:**
| | |
|---|---|
| Section 1 | 19 |
| Section 2 | 3 |
| Section 3 | 28 |
| Section 4 | 29 |
| Section 5 | 41 |
| Section 6 | 8 |
| Section 7 | 27 |
| Section 8 | 24 |
| Section 9 | 18 |
| Section 10 | 13 |
| Section 11 | 22 |
| Section 12 | 9 |
| Section 13 | 4 |
| Section 14 | 20 |
| Section 15 | 20 |
| Section 16 | 9 |
| Section 17 | 10 |
| Total Scotland | 304 |

| | |
|---|---|
| **England** | 4 |
| **Wales** | 8 |
| **Ireland** | 7 |
| **Furth of Scotland** | 19 |

| | |
|---|---|
| GRAND TOTAL | 323 |